Grand Diplôme Cooking Course

Volume 8

Grand Diplôme Cooking Course

A Danbury Press Book

The Danbury Press

a division of Grolier Enterprises, Inc.

Robert B. Clarke   Publisher

This book has been adapted from the Grand Diplôme Cooking Course, originally published by Purnell Cookery, U.S.A.

Purnell Grand Diplôme Editorial Board

Rosemary Hume and Muriel Downes Principals, London Cordon Bleu Cookery School, England

Anne Willan	Editor
Eleanor Noderer	Associate Editor
Sheryl Julian	Assistant Editor
John Paton	Managing Editor
José Northey	Co-ordinating Editor
Peter Leather	Art Editor
Charles F. Turgeon	Wine Consultant

Library of Congress Catalog Card Number: 72-13896
© B.P.C. Publishing, 1971, and
© Phoebus Publishing, 1972.
Filmsetting by Petty and Sons Ltd., Leeds, England.
Printed in the United States of America

23456789987

All recipes have been tested either at the Cordon Bleu Cookery School in London or in our U.S. test kitchens.

Note: all recipe quantities in this book serve 4 people unless otherwise stated.

Contents

From the Editor

A golden roast turkey, resplendent in its own juices, surrounded by spiced apples and glazed sweet potatoes, conjures up pleasing pictures of Thanksgivings past. But the practical **Ideas for Thanksgiving** in this Volume of your Grand Diplôme Cooking Course are very much part of the present.

There's advice from the London Cordon Bleu Cookery School on roasting turkey, capon and goose, with suggestions for accompaniments and how to prepare as much as possible ahead. Your favorite **Party Pies and Drinks** are not forgotten, and after the feast you can give new life to the **Leftovers** in dishes like turkey mousse and deviled goose. Then look to the future and leave some rich **Plum Puddings** and **Mincemeat** to mellow on the shelves in anticipation of Christmas.

Summer is the time to enjoy the sparkling delights of **Savory and Sweet Gelatins** ranging from simple tomato chartreuse and fresh lemon gelatin to the highlights of haute cuisine such as duck set with orange segments in a mold of wine-flavored aspic. Equally legendary are creations like vol-au-vent aux fruits de mer (a puff pastry case filled with shellfish in a creamy wine sauce) and palmiers (heart-shaped pastries, crisp with caramelized sugar) whose intricacies are made easy in the feature on **Puff Pastry.**

From France it is a short step to Italy with fragrant zuppa di vongole, fruit-topped cassata and other temptations of **Italian Cooking.** The second feature on **Pasta** — homemade lasagne, canneloni and gnocchi — completes the southern survey, and a serve-yourself **Pizza Party** brings you back home to America.

For more formal entertaining, the **Menus** in this Volume include an elegant buffet for 36 people, and three dinners designed for different seasons of the year.

Happy cooking and Bon Appétit!

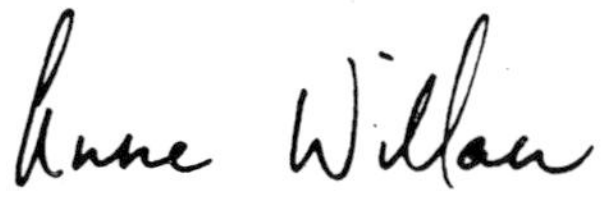

Anne Willan

For a colorful dinner, serve shoulder of veal hongroise with small new potatoes and cucumber Vichy (recipes on page 12)

A Dinner with a French Flair

The Riesling and other white wines of the drier sort from Yugoslavia are particularly interesting and would be ideal for this menu's appetizer — shrimps in aspic. Eastern European wines are becoming increasingly available here and their generally sound quality and low cost deserve attention.

A pleasant alternative from California, derived from Eastern European grapes, is the light and fresh-tasting Green Hungarian. For shoulder of veal, the Egri Bikavér from Hungary offers a hearty flavor in a red wine that is widely distributed, but instead you might want to try one of the new, non-traditional red wines from New York State — Baco Noir.

Shrimps in Aspic

Shoulder of Veal Hongroise
Buttered Noodles or Boiled New Potatoes
Cucumber Vichy

Pears Charcot

~~

White wine — Riesling (Yugoslavia)
or Green Hungarian (California)

Red wine — Egri Bikavér (Hungary)
or Baco Noir (New York)

TIMETABLE

Day before
Make the fish stock for aspic.

Morning
Clarify the aspic and prepare the shrimp molds.
Poach the pears in syrup; make vanilla cream mold and chill in the refrigerator.
Make the sauce for the pears.
Prepare tomatoes and pimientos.
Spread garlic mixture into the veal incisions.
Prepare potatoes, if serving.
Peel and cut the cucumbers, blanch and refresh.
Peel or scrape the carrots, put into a pan with butter, sugar, salt and water.
Chop the parsley and shallot.

Assemble equipment for final cooking from 6:00 for dinner around 8 p.m.

You will find that **cooking times** given in the individual recipes for these dishes have sometimes been adapted in the timetable to help you when cooking and serving this menu as a party meal.

Order of Work

6:00
Set oven at moderately hot (375°F).

6:15
Put the veal in oven.
Unmold shrimps in aspic onto a platter and garnish. Cut and butter the wholewheat bread to accompany the shrimps in aspic. Keep covered with plastic wrap.

6:30
Baste the veal and continue basting at 15 minute intervals.
Arrange the pears Charcot on a serving dish.

7:00
Turn the meat and baste again.

7:30
Start cooking the carrots, add cucumber and parsley; season with pepper when the water has evaporated, then toss. Keep warm.
Cook potatoes or noodles.

7:45
Place the meat on a platter. Put plates in oven to warm. Carve the meat, finish the sauce and spoon over the meat. Cover with foil and return meat to oven to keep warm. Drain potatoes or noodles and toss with butter.

8:00
Serve appetizer.

Appetizer

Shrimps in Aspic

¾ lb peeled, cooked medium shrimps
3 cups aspic, made with fish stock
buttered wholewheat bread (to serve)

For garnish
2–3 slices of canned pimiento, drained
bunch of chervil or parsley
bunch of watercress

8 dariole molds or small custard cups

The flavor of this dish will be best if you use homemade aspic. A recipe for this and for a quick version of aspic are given on pages 18–19.

Method
Prepare the aspic.
Place the molds or custard cups in a tray or roasting pan with about 1 inch of water and some ice cubes. Pour a layer of cool aspic, about ¼ inch deep, into the bottom of the molds and leave until set.
Cut a small circle of pimiento for each mold, dip the pimiento into a little of the liquid aspic and place in the center of the solidified aspic layer. Put a small sprig of chervil or parsley at each side of the pimiento circles. Gently pour 1 tablespoon aspic over the decoration to hold it in place. Chill until set.
Arrange the shrimps (reserving 8 for garnish) and aspic in layers (leaving the molds or cups in ice water until each layer is set) until the molds are full. Finish with a layer of aspic.

Pour a thin layer of aspic into a shallow cake or pie pan to use for decoration. Reserve any remaining aspic. Chill the molds and layer of aspic about 1–1½ hours in the refrigerator or until firm.
If serving the molds on a silver or stainless steel platter, pour a thin coating of the reserved cool but still liquid aspic over the bottom of the platter and chill until set. Loosen the shrimp molds by carefully dipping them quickly in and out of hot water. Unmold them on the aspic-coated platter. Coarsely chop the thin layer of aspic, and arrange around the turned-out molds.
Garnish with watercress and the reserved shrimps. Serve the shrimps in aspic with slices of buttered wholewheat bread.

Use a skewer to arrange the pieces of pimiento and sprigs of chervil or parsley on the layer of aspic

To speed up the setting process, layer the shrimps and aspic in the molds and stand them in a dish of ice water ▸

Shrimps in aspic are garnished with a few whole shrimps and a bunch of watercress

Entrée

Shoulder of Veal Hongroise

2½–3 lb shoulder of veal, boned,
   rolled and tied
2 cloves of garlic
2 teaspoons paprika
¼ cup butter
1 bay leaf
1 shallot, finely chopped
1½–2 cups veal or chicken
   stock
salt and pepper
1 red bell pepper, cored, seeded
   and sliced, or 2 slices of
   canned pimiento
1 tablespoon flour
3 medium tomatoes, peeled,
   seeded and cut into 8 pieces
¼ cup plain yogurt

Method
Crush the garlic to a paste
with the paprika and 1 tablespoon butter. With a sharp-
pointed knife, make about 12
incisions in the surface of the
veal and insert some of the
paste into each of these. Set
oven at moderately hot
(375°F).

Heat the remaining butter
in a roasting pan, put in the
meat and baste well with
butter. Add the bay leaf and
shallot, pour over 1½ cups
stock, sprinkle with a little
salt and pepper and roast in
heated oven for 1½ hours or
until tender. Baste every 15
minutes and turn meat over
halfway through roasting.

Blanch the red pepper for 1
minute in boiling water and
drain, or drain the pimiento
and cut into strips.

Remove the veal from the
roasting pan, slice and
arrange on a warm platter;
keep warm. Turn the oven
down to low (200°F).

Strain the liquid from the
roasting pan, measure it and
add enough extra stock or
water to measure 1½ cups.
Skim all fat from the top of
the liquid; mix the flour with a
little of the liquid to make a
smooth paste and stir it into
the remaining stock in a
saucepan. Bring to a boil,
stirring constantly, until
smooth. Add the prepared
tomato pieces and pepper or
pimiento strips and simmer
2–3 minutes. Taste for seasoning and spoon the sauce
over the slices of veal.

Beat the yogurt lightly with
a fork and spoon it over the
top of the meat. Cover securely with foil and return to the
warm oven for 15–20 min-
utes.

Serve with buttered nood-
les or small new potatoes,
boiled and tossed in butter.
Cucumber Vichy is also a
delicious accompaniment.

*1 Work the paste of butter,
paprika and garlic into the
veal so that the flavors pene-
trate the meat thoroughly
through the incisions*

*2 Before roasting, pour veal
or chicken stock over the veal
and add a bay leaf, chopped
shallot and a little salt and
pepper*

*3 Spoon yogurt over the veal
after it has been sliced and
covered with a sauce of tomatoes, pepper or pimientos and
stock*

1

2

3

Cucumber Vichy

2 cucumbers
4–5 carrots
1 tablespoon butter
1 teaspoon sugar
large pinch of salt
1 tablespoon chopped parsley
black pepper, freshly ground

Method
Peel the cucumbers, cut in
half lengthwise and then cut
across in ½ inch slices. Blanch
in boiling water for 1 minute,
drain, refresh under cold
running water and set aside.

Peel or scrape the carrots,
cut them in quarters and put
in a large pan with the butter,
sugar, salt and just enough
water to cover. Cook with the
lid on for 10 minutes or until
carrots are almost tender.

Remove the lid and con-
tinue cooking until the water
has evaporated. Add the
cucumber and parsley and
season with pepper. Toss the
vegetables gently until they
are coated with the butter,
sugar and parsley glaze.

*Toss the vegetables for
cucumber Vichy to coat them
with a delicious butter, sugar
and parsley glaze*

For pears charcot, pears are poached in syrup and arranged around a vanilla cream mold for serving

Dessert

Pears Charcot

4 ripe dessert pears
1½ cups water
¼ cup sugar
juice of ½ lemon
2 tablespoons apricot jam
1 cup quince or peach jam

For vanilla cream mold
2 cups milk
1 vanilla bean or 2–3 drops
   of vanilla extract
3 egg yolks
2 tablespoons sugar
1 envelope gelatin
5 tablespoons water
1 cup heavy cream, whipped
   until it holds a soft shape

*6 inch springform pan, or
soufflé dish (1 quart
capacity); pastry bag and
star tube*

Method

Lightly oil the springform pan or soufflé dish.

Put the water, sugar and lemon juice in a pan over low heat. When the sugar dissolves, boil the syrup for 3 minutes.

Pare the pears, cut in half, scoop out the cores with a teaspoon and immediately put the pears, rounded side down, in the hot syrup. Cover the pan and poach the pears over low heat for 15–20 minutes or until they are tender but still hold their shape. Let stand in the syrup to cool.

To make the vanilla cream mold: heat the milk with the vanilla bean (do not add vanilla extract now). Cover pan and let the milk stand about 15 minutes until it is well-flavored with vanilla. Remove vanilla bean. Beat the egg yolks with the sugar

until thick and light and gradually stir in the hot milk. Return the mixture to the pan and cook over low heat, stirring constantly, until the custard is thick enough to coat the back of a spoon. Add the vanilla extract if not using a vanilla bean. Strain the custard, cover and let stand until cool.

Sprinkle the gelatin over 5 tablespoons water in a small pan and let stand 5 minutes until spongy. Then dissolve over a pan of hot water and stir into the custard. Pour the

custard into a thin metal pan and stand in cold water to which some ice cubes have been added. Stir frequently until the custard begins to thicken creamily, then fold in half of the whipped cream. Pour the mixture into the prepared pan or soufflé dish and refrigerate at least 2 hours or until set.

Lift the pears out of the syrup onto a plate. Add both jams to the syrup in the pan and heat slowly until they are melted. Work through a sieve, then boil 2–3 minutes. Let this

sauce stand until cool.

Just before serving, loosen the sides of the vanilla cream mold with the tip of a small knife and turn out into a serving dish. Stiffly whip remaining cream and spoon it into the pastry bag fitted with the star tube. Then pipe straight lines on top of the mold. With remaining cream pipe rosettes around the top of the vanilla cream mold.

Arrange the pears, rounded side up, around the mold and coat with the sauce.

Beet gelatin salad is an ideal accompaniment to cold roast beef and horseradish cream (recipe is on page 27)

SAVORY AND SWEET GELATINS

Sparkling, clarified molds set with gelatin are one of the prides of French cuisine; they can be savory or sweet, and vary in color from crimson to brown to gold or bright yellow. When layered with fruit, eggs, chicken, meat or vegetables, they make meals in themselves, or they may be used to give a shiny, decorative coating to cold foods.

The basic sweet and savory clarified gelatins are lemon gelatin and aspic. They are not difficult to make, but time and attention to detail is needed to produce a brilliant crystal-clear gelatin. To do this, a mixture must be 'clarified', a term used in cooking to denote two completely different things – either the clearing of gelatins, as here, or the clearing and refining of butter, frying fat or drippings.

Gelatins are clarified with egg whites that are beaten into the mixture as it is heated so the whites coagulate to form a thick crust or 'filter'. Consommé and lemon gelatin are more difficult to clear than aspic, so raw shredded beef is added with the egg whites to help make a more solid 'filter' for consommé, while lightly crushed egg shells augment the egg whites for lemon gelatin.

The equipment needed for clarifying is simple: a large enamel or stainless steel pan or kettle with a ground base, a whisk, and a dish towel for aspics and consommés, or a jelly bag for making lemon or any fruit gelatin.

Aspics are stiffened or set either naturally, as in a firmly jellied stock, or by adding powdered gelatin. Stock that has become softly jellied must have some gelatin added and it is important to use just the right amount to give a good set; aspics that are too stiff are unpalatable. When making gelatins it is easiest to clear not less than 4 cups of liquid at a time – enough for 4 people. Any left over keeps well.

Not all molds set with gelatin need to be clarified. Colorful jellied vegetable or fruit salads make popular summer luncheon and supper dishes (see pages 27–29).

General Rules

Before you begin clarifying, make your pan or kettle, whisk, and dish towel or jelly bag scrupulously clean by scalding them. Fill the pan with cold water, put in the whisk and bring to a boil. Pour the water through the clean dish towel to scald it thoroughly, then wring it out and set aside. Scald two large bowls for straining.

Use a jelly bag by setting it up on a stand or hanging it between two chair backs. Put a bowl underneath the bag, then pour boiling water through it. Take the bowl of water and pour it through the bag again (having placed another bowl underneath the bag). After using, wash the bag well in warm water (no soap), scald it with boiling water and hang it up to dry.

For making aspic, use a good clear stock, preferably made with raw bones, that have been simmered slowly for a long time.

Place the cold stock or liquid in the scalded pan. If powdered gelatin is needed, add this to any wine or a small quantity of the cold measured liquid and let it stand until spongy before adding to the main liquid.

Whisk the egg whites only to a froth and add them to the liquid. Set the pan over moderate heat and whisk the whites again, moving the whisk backwards (the reverse of the usual) and down. This encourages the whites to mix down into the liquid and, when this boils, the whites will coagulate or curdle, causing the liquid to become opaque. (If you have ever curdled a custard you will recognize this stage.)

When the liquid is hot, add the soaked powdered gelatin and continue whisking until the liquid reaches boiling point.

Watchpoint: if the powdered gelatin is not previously soaked, there is a danger of the mixture sticking to the bottom of the pan during heating as it scorches easily.

As soon as the liquid boils, stop whisking and let the mixture boil well and rise in the pan. At once, turn off the heat or draw the pan aside and leave the liquid to settle for 5 minutes. Bring it back to a boil and remove the pan from the heat; do not whisk throughout this stage.

At this point the 'filter' of egg white will have cracked and the liquid below will be visible. It should look clear so that the next stage of straining can be carried out. If the liquid is muddy-looking, which may happen with any fruit gelatin, e.g. lemon, bring it to a boil once more.

To strain: carefully ladle the liquid with its 'filter' into the prepared dish towel (doubled, if a thin one) laid over a bowl or bag, hanging over a bowl. Allow about one-third to run through. Then, if using the dish towel, lift it up carefully and lay it over the second bowl. Pour the gelatin in the first bowl back onto the filter lying in the dish towel or bag. If the gelatin is not crystal clear after this straining, repeat the process.

When most of the gelatin has run through, the clearing procedure is continued by gathering up the sides of the dish towel, tying them together with string and suspending it from a hook (or suitable projection) to let the remaining gelatin drain. Alternatively, leave the cloth lying across the surface of the bowl, but slightly lifted, so it does not touch the liquid on the bottom.

When using a jelly bag the clearing procedure is the same. After the first cup has been drained through the bag, return the liquid to the bag and repeat this at frequent intervals until the gelatin runs clear. Never squeeze or force the liquid through the bag.

Gelatin runs more slowly through a bag than a cloth and it may reach setting point before it has all run through. To prevent this, fill a bottle or screwtop jar with hot water and place it carefully in the center of the bag, being careful not to spill any water. The warmth from the water will keep the gelatin liquid.

Aspic and most gelatins containing wine will keep for several days in the refrigerator. Pour the gelatin into a pitcher or bowl and chill until set. Cover with about $\frac{1}{2}$ inch cold water and refrigerate.

Watchpoint: don't forget to pour off the water before using the gelatin.

The best aspic is set with gelatin extracted from calves' feet during cooking (see page 25), and is especially delicate in flavor. Most **powdered gelatin** is obtained by boiling the bones or tissues of animals or fish.

One envelope of gelatin will set 1 pint (2 cups) of liquid. It is never added directly to a liquid but must be softened first: sprinkle the gelatin over a small quantity of liquid (the recipe will say how much) in a small pan. Leave it for 5 minutes or until it swells and looks spongy. Then dissolve it over a pan of hot water or add it to a warm mixture so it dissolves. When gelatin is completely dissolved, no trace of crystals can be seen when the mixture is lifted in a spoon.

A jelly bag is a cone-shaped bag made of close-textured cotton or linen. Some bags have a removable hoop to hold the top open and tapes for hanging.

A jelly bag is only essential for a fruit, e.g. lemon, gelatin; aspics and wine gelatins can be cleared satisfactorily through a cloth because they cloud less easily than fruit gelatins.

Points to remember when clarifying

1 The liquid or stock to be clarified should be well flavored, completely free from grease and semi-clear before clarification begins.

2 The stock used for aspic must be cold, first because it is easier to remove every trace of solidified fat from cold stock, and second because it is the slow coagulation of the egg whites being whisked through the cold stock as it comes to boiling point that produces a clear gelatin.

3 Use a large pan or kettle: the cold stock or liquid should not come more than one-third up the sides of the kettle to leave room for the contents to rise on boiling.

4 Once the mixture has come to a boil do not whisk while a crust is forming or you will break up this 'filter'. It must be ladled very gently into the cloth for straining.

5 Never squeeze the bag or cloth during straining but leave it to drain naturally.

To clarify gelatin, whisk egg white and stock over moderate heat; add gelatin when hot

Stop whisking when stock, egg white and gelatin mixture boils and let liquid rise

When clear, strain liquid into a bowl through its filter using a dish towel or jelly bag

Coating with Aspic

Temperature is the key to coping with aspic and it is easier, although not essential, to work in a cool kitchen around 50°F–60°F. The food to be coated or molds to be filled must be very cold so the aspic sets on contact with them. The aspic must be absolutely cold and on the point of setting when basted or brushed over food.

A refrigerator will chill food, platters and molds sufficiently for aspic work but this will take time, particularly in hot weather. If you have a freezer, use it, but do not leave food inside long enough to freeze. Once aspic has been added, take care, for it will crystallize if left in the freezer too long, and when thawed will melt to a puddle.

To cool the aspic, pour 1–2 cups into a small pan or metal bowl and set it over a pan of ice water. Stir the aspic very gently from time to time until it is very cold – do not stir vigorously or it will become cloudy with air bubbles. When about to set, the aspic will thicken slightly and become almost oily in consistency. Work fast at this stage, as it sets very quickly.

If aspic sets before you have finished filling the mold or coating food, warm it slightly until liquid and chill again over ice. Large platters of food with complicated decorations and garnishes may need two or three coatings of aspic. To do this, set the food on a wire rack with a tray underneath to catch drippings and give it one or more coatings, re-using any aspic that falls into the tray. Then arrange the food on a platter and give it a final, overall coating.

Basting. This method is used when food has been previously coated with a sauce or has a decoration of truffle, egg white etc., arranged on it. The best way is to take a large spoonful of cold aspic at a time and hold the spoon on an ice cube while stirring aspic gently with the little finger. When it feels ice cold, it will begin to thicken and is ready to baste over the food.

Brushing. This is a quick method, suitable only for plain, undecorated food like whole trout or salmon, fish steaks, sliced meats and whole or cut up chicken. Use a badger-hair brush (obtainable at art stores) or soft pastry brush, wash it thoroughly and scald it in boiling water so that it is absolutely clean before using.

Filling Molds

When filling small molds, spoon gelatin into the bottom to make a $\frac{1}{4}$ inch layer. Chill until set. To chill molds quickly, stand them in a shallow pan of ice water. When set, fill as indicated in the recipe. Carefully pour in 1 more tablespoon gelatin and chill again so it sets, securing the filling. Leave room between filling and side of the mold for gelatin to run down and give a good coating. Finally, fill the mold to the top with gelatin and chill until very firm, allowing at least $1\frac{1}{2}$–2 hours before unmolding.

Large molds are filled in the same way, but the filling may be added and set in several layers.

Turning out Molds

Small molds. Have a bowl of hand-hot water, a sheet of wax paper dampened with cold water, a metal spatula and prepared platter ready.

Grip the mold firmly with the palm of your hand over the top and gently swish it through the hot water once or twice.

Still holding the mold, turn it over so your palm is underneath and the mold on top. Sharply knock the mold with the fingers of your other hand until the contents drop onto your open palm.

Slide the gelatin gently onto the dampened paper before transferring it to the platter with the spatula.

Large molds. Lower the mold into a pan of hand-hot water so the water just reaches the top edge. Leave it a few seconds, easing the gelatin gently sideways with your fingers to make sure it is loose.

Lift out the mold and wipe off any water with a cloth. Hold the platter over the mold, then quickly turn both over together. Set the platter on the table and, holding both mold and platter firmly, give a sharp shake sideways. The gelatin will drop onto the platter.

Lift off the mold carefully and wipe around the edge of the platter before serving.

Decorating the Platter

All molded gelatins or foods brushed and coated with aspic look most effective on silver or stainless steel platters, on crystal or glass, or on plain white china perhaps with a plain gold edge.

If using silver or stainless steel platters, pour a thin coating of cool aspic onto the bottom of the platter and chill until it is set. Arrange small molds, or pieces of chicken, fish or meat on top of this.

Food set in or brushed with aspic can be kept in the refrigerator for up to a day without harm, provided it is covered so the surface of the aspic cannot dry out and toughen. Molded gelatins can be stored in their molds, covered, for up to 48 hours.

Chopped Gelatin

To make a garnish of savory or sweet chopped gelatin, pour a $\frac{1}{4}$–$\frac{1}{2}$ inch layer into a clean ice cube tray or cake pan that has been well dampened. Chill thoroughly until gelatin is set firmly, then turn out onto a piece of wet brown or silicone paper. Chop it with a knife, but do not hold the point down as is usual when chopping. Avoid touching gelatin with your hand as any trace of grease will cloud it. Tilt the edge of the paper occasionally to move the gelatin around and leave it coarsely chopped as it will sparkle more.

Layers of gelatin can also be cut into diamonds and triangles to garnish the edges of platters.

Chop gelatin on a piece of wet silicone paper for use as a garnish

Aspic

Aspic is a savory, clarified gelatin made from good fish, chicken or meat stock, very slightly sharpened with wine and a few drops of wine vinegar. The stock should be well flavored and seasoned with a pleasantly acid but not too sharp taste.

Homemade aspic adds to the flavor of delicate foods like fish, eggs and shrimps. However, if you need aspic only for brushing over sliced meat, you can make an easy substitute by using canned consommé with 1–2 tablespoons brandy or sherry for flavor.

Quick Aspic

1 can consommé
$\frac{1}{2}$ envelope gelatin
1–2 tablespoons brandy or sherry

Method
Sprinkle the gelatin over 3 tablespoons of the consommé in a small pan and let stand 5 minutes until spongy. Dissolve over gentle heat and stir into the remaining consommé with the brandy or sherry.

Basic Aspic

2 envelopes gelatin
$\frac{1}{4}$ cup sherry
$\frac{1}{4}$ cup white wine
$3\frac{1}{2}$ cups cold stock
1 teaspoon wine vinegar
2 egg whites

The amount of gelatin given in this recipe will set a liquid or very lightly jellied stock firmly enough to turn out of a mold.

Stock already set to a strong jellied consistency, e.g. that made with veal bones, needs less powdered gelatin, so cut the amount to $1\frac{1}{2}$ envelopes if the aspic is to be molded. For an aspic dish served on a platter — not molded — the amount of gelatin may be reduced even further or in some cases omitted, but this is specified in recipes.

Method
Sprinkle the gelatin over the sherry and wine in a small pan and leave 5 minutes until spongy. Pour the cold stock into a scalded pan or kettle and add the vinegar. Whisk the egg whites to a froth, add them to the pan, set it over moderate heat and whisk backwards (see general rules, page 16) until the stock is hot. Add the softened gelatin and continue whisking steadily until the mixture boils.

Stop whisking and let the liquid rise to the top of the pan; turn off heat or draw pan aside and leave to settle for about 5 minutes. Bring to a boil again, draw pan aside once more and leave liquid to settle. At this point the liquid seen through the egg white filter should look clear. If not, repeat the boiling process.

Filter the aspic through a cloth or jelly bag (see page 16) and cool before using.

Stocks for Aspic

The stock for aspic may be white (for chicken, veal or lamb), brown (for beef) or fish stock, depending on the dish being made and the color should vary accordingly — light gold for fish, chicken and white meats and rich brown for beef and game.

White Stock

1 lb veal bones
$\frac{1}{2}$ lb chicken backs or giblets (without liver)
$2\frac{1}{2}$ quarts water
1 onion, quartered
1 carrot, quartered
1 stalk of celery, sliced
bouquet garni
6 peppercorns
$\frac{1}{2}$ teaspoon salt

Use this stock for making aspic for chicken, veal or lamb.

Method
Wipe the bones and put them in a large pan with the chicken backs or giblets. Add the water and bring slowly to a boil; skim well. Add the vegetables, bouquet garni, peppercorns and salt to the pan, bring back to a boil and skim again. Half cover the pan and simmer gently for 2 hours. Strain and leave to cool.

Remove any small particles of fat floating on the surface by drawing a strip of paper towel over the top of the stock while it is still warm.

When the stock is cold, cover and store it in the refrigerator for up to 3 days.

Brown Stock

1 lb beef bones
1 lb boneless shin of beef
$2\frac{1}{2}$ quarts water
1 onion, quartered
1 carrot, quartered
2 stalks of celery, sliced
bouquet garni
6 peppercorns
$\frac{1}{2}$ teaspoon salt

Use this stock for making aspic for beef or game.

Method
Wipe the bones, put them in a roasting pan and bake in a moderately hot oven (375°F) for 30 minutes or until very brown. Meanwhile chop the beef finely and reserve.

Lift the bones from the roasting pan with a slotted spoon and put them into a large pan or kettle. Add the water with the beef and bring slowly to a boil; skim well. Add the vegetables, bouquet garni, peppercorns and salt; half cover the pan and simmer gently for about 3 hours.

Strain the stock into a bowl and cool, removing any fat particles as for white stock. Cover and store in the refrigerator for up to 3 days.

Fish Stock

$1\frac{1}{2}$ lb fish bones
1 medium onion, sliced
1 tablespoon butter
6 white peppercorns
small bouquet garni
juice of $\frac{1}{2}$ lemon
salt
5 cups water

Method
Blanch the onion and refresh it. Wash the fish bones and drain.

Melt the butter in a large pan or kettle, add the onion, fish bones, peppercorns, bouquet garni, lemon juice and salt. Cover the pan and cook over very gentle heat for 10 minutes. Add the water, bring to a boil and skim well. Simmer gently for 20 minutes, then strain through a fine nylon strainer.

Cool, cover and store in the refrigerator for up to 2 days.

Consommé

The method for making and clarifying consommé is similar to that for aspic. Homemade consommé calls for specially strong stock made from beef or chicken, depending on the kind of consommé you want to `make. It may be served plain, or with julienne strips of chicken or game as a simple garnish. Consommé can also be flavored with tomato (consommé madrilène) or beet (consommé bortsch). These recipes will be given in a future Volume.

Basic Consommé

2 quarts beef or chicken stock
¾ lb lean boneless shin of beef, finely shredded
¼ cup sherry or Madeira
whites and shells (wiped and crushed) of 2 eggs
extra sherry or Madeira (to taste) – optional

Method
Put the stock into a thick enamel, stainless steel or tin-lined pan or kettle. (Using a metal whisk with any other type of pan will make a stock cloudy.) Add the beef and sherry or Madeira.

Whip the egg whites to a light froth and add to the liquid with the crushed shells. Whisk backwards over moderate heat (see general rules, page 16) until the liquid boils. Stop whisking and allow the liquid to rise to the top of the pan. Draw it aside for about 5 minutes, then carefully boil it again, taking care not to break up the 'filter' that forms on the top. Lower heat and leave to cook very slowly for 40 minutes to extract all

the flavor from the meat.

Place a scalded dish towel over a bowl and pour the liquid through, at first keeping the 'filter' back with a spoon and then, at the end, sliding it out onto the cloth. Pour the liquid again through the 'filter' and the cloth. The consommé should now be clear. If it is not, pour it again through the cloth. Add extra sherry or Madeira, if you like, and any garnish called for in the recipe. Reheat the consommé but do not boil.

If serving the consommé chilled, it should set to a light jellied consistency. Just before serving stir lightly with a fork to break it up and then spoon it into bowls.

Beef Stock for Consommé

1½ lb beef bones
1½ lb veal bones
1½ lb lean beef
½ tablespoon oil
1–2 carrots, sliced
1–2 onions, sliced
1 stalk of celery, sliced
bouquet garni
6 peppercorns
½ teaspoon salt
3½ quarts cold water (to cover generously)

Method
Have the butcher cut the bones into small pieces. Cut the beef into 1 inch squares, put in a pan or kettle with the bones and brown in the oil. Lower the heat, add the vegetables and brown them also. Add the remaining ingredients and bring slowly to a boil, skimming well. Partly cover the pan with a lid and simmer 2–3 hours or until the stock is strong in flavor. Strain, cool, cover and chill overnight. Remove all fat.

Note: alternatively 3–4 lb rump or plate of beef may be simmered until tender (in water to cover) with 2–3 veal bones and quartered root vegetables. The meat and vegetables are served as an entrée and the broth is left to simmer uncovered until the flavor is concentrated. Then strain it and use as a base for consommé, aspic and brown sauces.

Chicken Stock for Consommé

Make as above with veal bones but substitute the raw carcass bones of a chicken or small fowl for the lean beef and beef bones.

SAVORY GELATINS

Oeufs à l'Estragon
(Eggs with Tarragon)

4–5 small eggs
about 4 cups chicken aspic, cool but still liquid
fresh tarragon leaves or parsley sprigs (for garnish)
¼ lb thinly sliced ham (optional)

4–5 ramekins or deep individual dishes

Make this dish with chicken aspic that is only lightly set – it is a delicious summer appetizer. If served as an entrée, double the quantities.

Method
To poach the eggs: in a deep skillet or shallow saucepan

heat 4 cups water with 1 tablespoon vinegar. When the water is boiling hard, break an egg into a patch of water that is boiling fast – the bubbles will spin the egg and help to keep it together.

Add the remaining eggs in the same way, turn down the heat at once and simmer the eggs gently for 3½–4½ minutes or until the whites are set and the yolks are still soft. Lift them out with a slotted spoon and keep in a bowl of cold water until needed.

Have ready the aspic and the ramekins or dishes.

Dip the tarragon leaves or parsley sprigs in boiling water for 1 second and drain them. Drain the eggs and dry carefully on paper towels; trim them, if necessary, and place each one in a ramekin or dish.

If you like, shred the ham and put a layer at the bottom of each dish; add a little cold aspic and chill until set. Then add the eggs.

Pour a little aspic into a small saucepan or metal bowl and stand it in ice water. Stir the aspic gently with a metal spoon until just cold but not set, then spoon enough into each dish to cover the egg. Arrange 2–3 tarragon leaves or parsley sprigs on top and chill until the aspic is set. Fill to the brim with remaining aspic that is on the point of setting. Cover and chill until served.

Oeufs en Gelée
(Eggs in Aspic)

4 small eggs
4 cups chicken aspic, cool but
  still liquid
4 thin slices of ham
1 small Boston lettuce or
  chopped aspic (for garnish –
  see chopped gelatin,
  page 18)

*4 oval eggs-in-aspic or large
  dariole molds (2½ inches
  deep)*

These are soft-cooked eggs
(oeufs mollets) rolled in slices
of ham and set in special
individual molds designed to
hold one egg each, with aspic
and garnish.

Method
Soft cook the eggs in their
shells by simmering them in
water to cover for 7 minutes.
Plunge them into cold water
and, when cool, peel them
carefully and keep in cold
water until needed.

Have the aspic ready and
pour enough into each mold
to make a three-eighths inch
layer. Stand the molds in a
roasting pan of ice water and
leave to set.

Drain the eggs, dry them
thoroughly and wrap each one
in a slice of ham. Put them in
the molds and fill to the brim
with aspic. Cover and chill
until set.

Just before serving, turn
the eggs out onto a platter or
onto individual plates, and
garnish with lettuce leaves or
chopped aspic.

Watchpoint: use small eggs
for this dish so they do not
rise above the edges of the
molds, thus preventing them
from sitting flat when turned
out.

Lamb Chops
in Mint Aspic

3 lb rack of lamb, chine bone
  removed
1 onion, sliced or quartered
1 carrot, sliced or quartered
1 stalk of celery, sliced or
  quartered

For aspic
4 cups white stock
2 envelopes gelatin (less if
  stock is firmly jellied)
2 teaspoons tarragon vinegar
bunch of mint
2 egg whites

Method
In a pan or kettle combine the
lamb with the vegetables to
flavor and water to cover.
Cover the pan and simmer
40–45 minutes or until the
lamb is tender. Cool in the
liquid.

To make the aspic: sprinkle
the gelatin over ½ cup stock
with the tarragon vinegar and
let stand 5 minutes until
spongy. Bruise 3 sprigs of
mint and add them to the pan
with the remaining stock and
egg whites, whisked to a
froth. Whisk backwards until
the liquid is hot; add the
softened gelatin. Continue
whisking until the mixture
boils. Draw the pan aside
and leave the liquid to settle
for 5 minutes. Re-boil if necessary, then pour the liquid
through a scalded dish towel
until clear. Cool.

Finely chop remaining mint
(there should be about 1
tablespoon) and add it to the
aspic.

Drain the meat, trim away
any fat and carve into chops.
Trim the ends of the chops
to expose about 1½ inches of
the bone.

Pour two-thirds of the aspic
into a deep platter and chill
until set. Arrange the chops
flat or overlapping on top of

Lamb chops are complemented by a delicate mint aspic

the aspic. Chill thoroughly.

Chill the remaining aspic
and, when on the point of
setting, spoon over the chops
to coat them.

Serve with small new
potatoes in mayonnaise and
peas and carrot salad. Use
this salad to garnish the
platter, or serve it separately,
as you like.

Peas and Carrot
Salad

Use cooked peas and whole
baby carrots or quartered
young carrots, cooked. Allow
about two-thirds quantity of
cooked peas to carrots. Toss
the vegetables with vinaigrette
dressing (see page 27) not
more than 5–10 minutes
before serving so the peas do
not discolor.

Roulades of Ham

8 thin slices of ham
⅓ cup rice
1 large can (9¼ oz) tuna, drained
3 slices of canned pimiento,
  drained and chopped
¾ cup mayonnaise
about 4 cups chicken or veal
  aspic, cool but still liquid

Method
Boil the rice in salted water
for 12 minutes or until just
tender; drain, rinse and dry.
Flake the tuna with a fork and
add to the rice with the
pimiento and enough mayonnaise to bind the mixture.

Spread the ham slices on a
board, divide the mixture
between them and roll them
up like fat cigars. Arrange in
a deep platter and chill.

Have the aspic ready and
pour it carefully onto the
platter to cover the roulades
completely. Cover and chill
until set and serve with your
choice of salad.

For a decorative entrée, serve a chartreuse of baby vegetables

Chartreuse of Baby Vegetables

1 bunch of small carrots
1 lb asparagus
3–4 medium tomatoes, peeled and cored
½ lb green beans
¾ lb baby lima beans
4 cups chicken aspic, cool but still liquid
2 cups cooked chicken, cut in strips

8–9 inch springform pan

This is a decorative entrée for a buffet lunch or supper. For a lighter dish, it may be made with vegetables only. Use any vegetables in season, providing they contrast well in color and flavor. To save time you can use canned consommé instead of chicken aspic although the flavor will not be as delicate. To each can of consommé add ½ envelope gelatin and 1–2 tablespoons brandy or sherry (see recipe for quick consommé on page 18).

Method

Trim and peel the carrots, leaving ¼ inch of the green top or, if large, slice them. Boil the carrots in salted water until barely tender; drain and refresh.

Trim the asparagus stalks, tie them together and cook, covered, in 1–2 inches of boiling salted water in an asparagus cooker or tall pan with stalks upright, so that the bottoms cook in water and the tops are steamed. After 8–10 minutes or when tender, drain and refresh.

Cut the tomatoes in quarters and scoop out the seeds. Trim the green beans, cut in half and boil in salted water for 12–15 minutes or until tender. Drain and refresh. Shell the lima beans and cook as for green beans 15–20 minutes or until tender.

Be sure the springform pan is very clean. Spoon a ¼–½ inch layer of aspic into the bottom of the pan and chill until set. Arrange the vegetables and chicken on the aspic to make a pattern (as shown in the photograph on opposite page).

Alternatively, start with an outer ring of the quartered tomatoes, add an inner ring of asparagus, then carrots, green beans and finally the limas. Spoon over just enough aspic to set the vegetables and chill. When set, add the chicken and remaining aspic so that it barely covers the top.

Cover and chill at least 1½ hours until very firm. Unmold just before serving and serve with a potato salad.

Near Grenoble, France, there is a Carthusian monastery called **La Grande Chartreuse.** The monks there are vegetarians, and they invented a vegetable dish which they made and cooked in molds — some very elaborate — and ate hot or cold. Thus all dishes of this kind are called a Chartreuse including those with meat, game and poultry, although correctly, the name should be given only to vegetarian dishes.

Fillets of Sole in Aspic

4 medium fillets of sole
1½ cups court bouillon
4–5 cups fish aspic, cool but still liquid

For filling
2 tablespoons butter
2 tablespoons flour
¾ cup milk
½ cup cooked, chopped shellfish (lobster, shrimps or crab)
squeeze of lemon juice
salt and pepper
1 egg yolk

For garnish
1 hard-cooked egg, sliced
1 truffle or 1 slice of canned pimiento, drained
chopped aspic (see chopped gelatin, page 18)
bunch of watercress
1 cucumber, peeled (optional)

4 large dariole molds

Method

To make the filling: in a saucepan melt the butter, stir in the flour off the heat and pour on the milk. Bring to a boil, stirring, and simmer 2 minutes. Take from heat and add the shellfish, lemon juice, salt and pepper to taste. Stir in the egg yolk, cook the mixture for 1–2 minutes over gentle heat to bind it and cool.

Spread the filling over the fish fillets, cutting them in half if they are large, and roll them up neatly. Tie loosely with string, set in a baking dish, pour over the court bouillon and cover with buttered foil. Poach in a moderate oven (350°F) for 10–12 minutes or until the fish flakes easily when tested with a fork. Drain, cool the fish rolls and remove string.

Pour a layer of aspic into the molds and chill until set. Arrange a decoration of sliced egg and truffle or pimiento on the bottom and set with another thin layer of aspic, adding it gradually and allowing each portion to set before adding the next. Cover and chill thoroughly.

Pour a thin layer of aspic onto an oval silver platter and chill until set. Unmold the fillets and arrange in a slanting line on the aspic. Garnish with chopped aspic, watercress and, if you like, sliced or diced cucumber.

Court bouillon: for 4 cup quantity, combine 4 cups water, 1 sliced carrot, 1 small onion (sliced and stuck with a clove), bouquet garni, 6 peppercorns and 2 tablespoons vinegar or lemon juice in a pan with a little salt. Cover, bring to a boil and simmer 15–20 minutes. Strain and use.

Molded Duck with Orange

4–5 lb duck
salt and pepper
2 teaspoons honey
2–3 tablespoons oil
3 large navel oranges
4–5 cups meat aspic, cool but still liquid (made with brown stock)
bunch of watercress (for garnish)

8 inch moule à manqué or springform pan (2–2½ quart capacity)

Method

Set oven at moderately hot (375°F).

Season inside the duck well with salt and pepper and spread the honey over the breast. Heat the oil in a roasting pan, put in the duck on a rack, baste it well, draining excess fat from the pan, and turn it from time to time so it browns evenly.

Roast the duck for 1½ hours or until no pink juice runs out when the thigh is pierced with a fork. When cooked, take from oven and cool.

Cut the rind and white pith from the oranges with a serrated-edge knife and section them. Pour a ¼ – ½ inch layer of aspic into the moule à manqué or springform pan and chill until set. Arrange the drained sections of orange in the pan and set them with a little more aspic.

Slice the breast and wing meat from the cooled duck, detach the legs and take out the bones. Cut the meat into neat slices and arrange them on the orange slices. Fill the pan to the top with remaining cool aspic, cover and chill at least 1½ hours until set. Just before serving, turn out mold and garnish with a bunch of watercress.

For a colorful buffet dish, serve cold roast duck, sliced and layered with oranges, then set in sparkling aspic

Arrange duck on the orange sections already set with aspic

A **moule à manqué** is a French cake pan with sloping as opposed to straight sides, often used for gelatin molds because they are less likely to collapse while unmolding.

It is said to have been named by a Paris pâtissier who criticized a cake mixture made by his chief baker. The baker, who didn't like his cake called a failure (un manqué), added butter, covered the cake with praline, and sold it to a customer — who came back for more! It was thus christened 'un manqué', and a special mold was designed for it.

SWEET GELATINS

Lemon Gelatin

2 envelopes gelatin
3 cups water
rind of 2 lemons
¾ cup lemon juice
2 sticks of cinnamon
¾ cup sugar
whites and shells (wiped and lightly crushed) of 2 eggs
¼ cup sherry or water

This basic recipe makes 4 cups gelatin.

Method

Sprinkle the gelatin over ½ cup water and let stand 5 minutes until spongy. Pour remaining water into a scalded pan, add the lemon rind and juice, cinnamon and sugar and heat gently until sugar is dissolved. Cool to tepid.

Whisk the egg whites to a froth and add to the pan with the egg shells, softened gelatin and sherry or water. Whisk this mixture backwards until the liquid reaches boiling point. Bring to a boil three times, drawing the pan aside for 5 minutes between each boiling to let the mixture settle.

Have a scalded jelly bag with a bowl underneath ready and ladle the contents of the pan into it. When the gelatin begins to run through, take away the bowl, placing another one underneath; pour the gelatin back into the bag. After it has run through a few times, it should be crystal clear. Let it run through completely before moving the bag; this may take 1 hour or more. If the gelatin in the bag starts to set, place a screwtop jar or a bottle of hot water in the center of the bag.

Calves' Feet Gelatin

For stock
2 calves' feet
3 quarts cold water

For clarifying each quart of stock
$\frac{1}{2}$ cup lemon juice
1 cup sherry
10 tablespoons sugar
4 whole cloves
1 stick of cinnamon
rind of 2 lemons
whites and shells (wiped and lightly crushed) of 2 eggs
$\frac{1}{2}$ cup brandy
a little powdered gelatin (if stock is not very firm)

This gelatin, with its sweet flavoring, was originally given to invalids because of its nutritional value. This quantity will fill about six 8 oz jars.

Method

Have the butcher cut the calves' feet into 5–6 pieces. Remove all the marrow and fat. Wash the feet well in warm water and scrape them. Put the pieces into a large pan or kettle, cover with cold water and bring to a boil. Drain and rinse well in cold water to clean thoroughly.

Return the pieces to the rinsed pan, add 3 quarts cold water and bring slowly to a boil. Simmer 5–6 hours or until the liquid is reduced by about one-third. Strain the stock through cheesecloth or a very fine sieve.

When cool, remove all fat from the stock. Measure the stock and put all ingredients for clarifying, except the brandy, into a large, deep pan. If extra gelatin is needed, soak it first in the sherry. Clarify the mixture as for lemon gelatin, adding the brandy just after straining for the first time.

Put the clear gelatin into clean, dry glass jars, cover and keep them in a cool place or in the refrigerator for up to 2 weeks.

Fruit Gelatin Flan

French flan pastry, made with
1$\frac{1}{4}$ cups flour, pinch of salt,
6 tablespoons butter,
6 tablespoons sugar, 3 egg yolks and $\frac{1}{2}$ teaspoon vanilla

For fruit gelatin
3–4 cups lemon gelatin, cool but still liquid
1–1$\frac{1}{2}$ cups fresh fruit in season (e.g. black and green grapes, bananas, strawberries, orange sections)

For pastry cream
$\frac{3}{4}$ cup milk
2 egg yolks
1 teaspoon cornstarch
2 tablespoons sugar
$\frac{3}{4}$ cup heavy cream, whipped until it holds a stiff peak

9 inch flan ring; 8 inch cake pan

This is a decorative dessert, especially when made in large quantities for a buffet. If you increase the recipe, remember that the cake pan must be slightly smaller than the flan ring, so the gelatin fits snugly on top of the cream filling in the pastry shell.

Method

To make French flan pastry dough: sift the flour with the salt onto a board or marble slab and make a large well in the center. Add the butter, sugar, egg yolks and vanilla and work together with the fingertips until smooth Gradually draw in the flour, working with the whole hand to form a smooth dough. Chill 1 hour.

Roll out the pastry dough, line flan ring and bake blind in a moderately hot oven (375°F) for 15–20 minutes or until the pastry is lightly browned. Remove the shell from the ring when cool.

Pour the gelatin into the cake pan to a depth of $\frac{1}{4}$ inch and chill until set. Arrange the chosen fruit on this and set it in position with a few tablespoons of cool gelatin. Chill until set. Repeat with another layer of fruit and when the fruit is set in place, fill the pan to the brim with the remaining gelatin. Cover and chill at least 1$\frac{1}{2}$ hours until the gelatin is very firm.

To make the pastry cream: scald the milk. Beat the egg yolks, cornstarch and sugar until light. Stir in the hot milk, return the mixture to the pan and bring to a boil, stirring. Cook 2 minutes, take from heat, cover pan tightly

with plastic wrap to prevent a skin from forming and leave to cool. When cold, fold in the whipped cream and spread the mixture on the bottom of the flan shell.

Dip the sides and base of the cake pan in warm water and carefully turn the gelatin out onto the cream in the flan shell. Chill the flan before serving.

Turn fruit gelatin flan out onto pastry cream already spread on bottom of the flan shell

Fruit gelatin flan has rings of halved grapes and bananas

Fruit Gelatin Madeleine

2½–3 cups lemon gelatin, cool
  but still liquid
1 cup fresh fruit in season
  (e.g. black grapes, cherries
  or strawberries)

For vanilla cream
2 egg yolks
2 teaspoons sugar
¾ cup milk
½ envelope gelatin
3–4 tablespoons water
½ teaspoon vanilla
½ cup heavy cream, whipped
  until it holds a soft shape

*Charlotte mold or bowl (4–5
cup capacity)*

Method
Pour a ¼–½ inch layer of
lemon gelatin into the mold
or bowl. Arrange the prepared
fruit on this and set it with a
little more gelatin, reserving
half.

To make the vanilla cream:
beat the egg yolks with sugar
until thick and light. Scald the
milk, pour onto the eggs, return the mixture to the pan
and stir over gentle heat until
the custard thickens enough
to coat the back of the spoon.
Do not boil or it will curdle.
Sprinkle the gelatin over the
water in a small pan, let stand
5 minutes until spongy. Dissolve over a pan of hot water.
Stir softened gelatin into the
custard with the vanilla. Stir
the custard over a bowl of ice
water until it is cold and on
the point of setting. Fold in
the whipped cream. Pour
carefully onto the jellied fruit
and chill until set.

Add any leftover fruit to
some of the remaining gelatin
and spoon over the top to fill
the mold or bowl completely.
Cover and chill the Madeleine
at least 1½ hours or until
firm. Chill remaining gelatin

until set and chop. Just
before serving, turn out mold;
surround with chopped gelatin.

Banana Chartreuse

4 cups lemon gelatin, cool but
  still liquid
12 pistachios (optional)
3 bananas
½ cup heavy cream, whipped
  until it holds a stiff peak
  (to serve)

Ring mold (1½ quart capacity)

Method
Have the gelatin ready, stand
the mold in a roasting pan and
pour around ice water.

Spoon a ¼–½ inch layer of
gelatin into the mold and leave
until set. Blanch the pistachios
in boiling water for 2 minutes,
drain and halve them. Cut the
bananas in ½ inch slices.
Place the pistachios on the
layer of gelatin, pour a little
more gelatin on top and leave
until set.

Dip the banana slices in
gelatin and arrange in a single
layer on top of the gelatin;
set this with a little more
gelatin and repeat the process
until the mold is full, making
the last layer gelatin. Pour
remaining gelatin into a damp
ice tray. Chill until firmly set.

Just before serving, unmold
the chartreuse and fill the center with chopped lemon gelatin. Serve a bowl of whipped
cream separately.

Sparkling banana chartreuse is served with whipped cream

*Dip the banana slices in gela-
tin to help them stick before
adding them to pan*

MOLDED SALADS

Savory uncleared gelatins are an American creation. They are quick to make and can be set in a ring or charlotte mold or in individual dariole molds. Try them as a colorful addition to a cold buffet or they are equally delicious as appetizers. Serve them with mayonnaise or vinaigrette dressing and hot garlic or herb French bread or buttered wholewheat bread.

Spiced Mushroom Mold

2 cups ($\frac{1}{2}$ lb) mushrooms
1 envelope gelatin
1 can consommé
2 teaspoons soy sauce
dash of Tabasco
dash of Worcestershire sauce
1 cup water
salt and pepper
squeeze of lemon juice

For garnish
lettuce leaves
lemon quarters
buttered wholewheat bread

7 inch square cake pan (1 quart capacity)

Method
Sprinkle the gelatin over $\frac{1}{4}$ cup consommé and let stand 5 minutes until spongy.

Trim the stems of the mushrooms level with the caps and wipe caps, if necessary. Chop the stems and combine in a pan with the remaining consommé, the sauces, water, mushroom caps and a little salt and pepper. Simmer 5–8 minutes or until the mushrooms are just tender.

Take from the heat and stir in the softened gelatin. Add lemon juice and taste for seasoning. Pour into the wet pan, cover and chill at least $1\frac{1}{2}$ hours until firmly set.

To serve, cut the salad into squares and arrange on lettuce leaves on individual plates. Garnish with lemon quarters and serve with wholewheat bread.

Beet Gelatin Salad

1 medium can (1 lb) sliced beets
$\frac{3}{4}$ cup juice from 1 can (16 oz) raspberries
2 teaspoons red wine vinegar
salt and pepper
2 envelopes gelatin

Ring mold (1 quart capacity)

This salad is good served with cold roast beef and horseradish cream.

Method
Drain the liquid from the beets and raspberries, mix juices with the vinegar and add seasoning. Measure 4 cups liquid, adding water if necessary. Sprinkle the gelatin over $\frac{1}{2}$ cup of this liquid and let stand 5 minutes until spongy; dissolve it over a pan of hot water. Stir into the remaining liquid and cool.

Arrange the beets in the wet mold. Pour over the cooled liquid, cover and chill at least $1\frac{1}{2}$ hours or until firmly set. Unmold the salad just before serving.

Vinaigrette Dressing

For every tablespoon vinegar (red or white wine, cider or tarragon) use 3 tablespoons olive or peanut oil. Mix in $\frac{1}{4}$ teaspoon each of salt and freshly ground black pepper, and chopped fresh herbs (thyme, marjoram, basil, or parsley).

Cucumber Gelatin Salad

2 cucumbers
1 envelope gelatin
2 cups chicken stock
$\frac{1}{2}$ cup heavy cream
$\frac{1}{2}$ teaspoon paprika
salt and pepper
1 cup backfin crab meat
$\frac{1}{4}$ cup vinaigrette dressing
1 tablespoon ketchup
3 medium tomatoes, peeled, cored and sliced

Ring mold (5 cup capacity)

Method
Peel the cucumbers, cut in half lengthwise, scoop out the seeds and dice the flesh. Blanch in boiling salted water for 1 minute, drain and refresh.

Sprinkle the gelatin over $\frac{1}{4}$ cup of the stock in a small pan and let stand 5 minutes until spongy; dissolve over a pan of hot water. Stir into remaining stock, add the cream and season well with paprika and salt and pepper to taste. Chill and, when on the point of setting, stir in the cucumber. Pour into the wet mold, cover and chill $1\frac{1}{2}$ hours or until firmly set.

Unmold onto a platter and fill the center with crab meat, mixed with vinaigrette dressing and ketchup. Surround salad with the tomatoes and chill before serving.

This salad may also be served without the crab meat; instead, garnish the center with watercress.

Molded Grape Salad

¾ lb seedless green grapes
2 envelopes gelatin
3 cups water
2 teaspoons chopped mint
½ cup lemon juice
sugar (to taste)
green food coloring (optional)

For serving
bunch of watercress
½ cup vinaigrette dressing
   (see page 27)
buttered wholewheat bread

Ring mold (1 quart capacity)

This salad should be pleasantly acid in flavor.

Method
Sprinkle the gelatin over ½ cup water and let stand 5 minutes until spongy; dissolve it over a pan of hot water. Add the remaining 2½ cups water, mint and lemon juice and sweeten to taste with sugar. Add a little coloring if you like.

Pour enough lemon mixture into the wet mold to make a ½ inch layer and chill until set. Put in the grapes and add enough lemon mixture to set them. Chill again until set, then fill the mold to the brim with the remaining lemon mixture. Cover and chill at least 1½ hours until very firm.

Unmold the salad onto a platter, garnish the center with watercress and serve vinaigrette dressing and buttered wholewheat bread separately.

Mousses Marie-Christina

1 can (5 oz) pâté de foie gras
   (goose liver pâté)
2 tablespoons butter, softened
salt and pepper
pinch of dry mustard
1 tablespoon heavy cream
½ envelope gelatin
2 cups aspic (flavored before
   clarifying with ¼ cup port
   instead of white wine and
   sherry)
¾ cup light cream
1 tablespoon Worcestershire
   sauce
2 teaspoons ketchup
½ cup shredded ham

4 ramekins or individual deep dishes

Method
Beat the pâté with the butter, season to taste, add the mustard and the heavy cream. Spread at the bottom of each ramekin or dish.

Sprinkle the gelatin over ¼ cup of the aspic, let stand 5 minutes until spongy. Dissolve over a pan of hot water and stir into the light cream. Add the Worcestershire sauce and ketchup with seasoning to taste and chill, stirring occasionally.

When on the point of setting, spoon the mixture into the ramekins or dishes to fill them threequarters full. Chill until set, cover with the ham and add the remaining aspic to fill completely. Cover and chill. Serve in the ramekins or dishes.

Tomato Chartreuse

4 cups (2 lb) canned tomatoes
strip of lemon rind
1 teaspoon tomato paste
1 clove of garlic, crushed
1 bay leaf
6 peppercorns
sugar (to taste)
salt and pepper
2 envelopes gelatin
½ cup white wine, or water

Suggested garnish
baby carrots and turnips;
   scallions; radishes; celery;
   green peas; lima beans; new
   potatoes
vinaigrette dressing
   (see page 27)
chopped mint or parsley
Dijon-style mustard
grated rind of ½ orange
8 thin slices of ham (for ham
   rolls)
1 package (3 oz) cream cheese
   mixed with ¼ cup chopped
   walnuts, or ¼ cup cooked
   shrimps and 1 tablespoon
   chopped canned pimiento
bunch of watercress
mayonnaise (to serve)

Ring mold (1 quart capacity)

Method
In a saucepan combine the tomatoes with their juice, lemon rind, tomato paste, garlic, bay leaf, peppercorns, and salt and sugar to taste. Bring slowly to a boil, simmer 3–4 minutes and work through a nylon strainer.

Sprinkle the gelatin over the wine or water in a small pan and let stand 5 minutes until spongy, then stir into the hot tomato mixture until gelatin is dissolved. Taste for seasoning and pour into the wet ring mold. Cover and chill at least 1½ hours or until firmly set.

Cook and dress the vegetables as follows:

Carrots: leave whole or trim into barrel shapes. Cook in boiling salted water until tender. Drain, refresh and cool. Dress with 2–3 tablespoons vinaigrette dressing mixed with 1 tablespoon chopped mint.
Turnips: cut in quarters and cook as for carrots. Dress with 3–4 tablespoons vinaigrette dressing mixed with 2 teaspoons Dijon-style mustard and grated rind of ½ orange.
Scallions: wash, trim and serve raw, or blanch them for 1 minute in boiling water.
Radishes: cut into roses and soak for about 1 hour in ice water.
Celery: cut into sticks and dress as for turnips.
Green peas: cook in boiling salted water until tender. Drain and refresh. Dress with vinaigrette dressing, sweetened with a little sugar; add chopped mint if you like.
Lima beans: cook as for peas. Dress with vinaigrette dressing.
Potatoes: cook and dress as for carrots, adding chopped mint or parsley if you like.

Unmold the chartreuse onto a large platter and surround with the dressed vegetables. Spread the cream cheese mixed with walnuts, or shrimps and pimiento, on the ham slices, roll up and place in center of mold. Add a bunch of watercress and serve a bowl of mayonnaise or vinaigrette dressing separately.
Note: julienne strips of chicken, bound with mayonnaise, may be substituted for the ham rolls.

Tomato chartreuse, garnished with cooked vegetables, is a colorful and decorative main dish

THE CORRECT MOLD

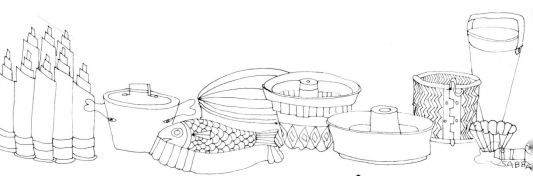

The array of molds available today is almost limitless. Kitchen specialty shops, department stores and mail-order houses that specialize in accessories for cooks offer a tremendous selection and new shapes are added every year.

As well as the triumph at the moment of unmolding, decorative molds themselves are an inspiration to the cook when displayed along a shelf, across a wall or all over a pegboard.

The most common molds are made of aluminum or anodized aluminum, the latter a coppery color in imitation of the old-fashioned copper ones. (In some stores real copper molds lined with tin are still available, but if they are of poor quality, the tin will melt when exposed to high temperatures.)

Aluminum has freed the imagination of the mold makers; practically any shape and size of mold is available in this versatile material.

Certain molds are traditional for certain dishes — charlotte russe, for instance, would be just another cream dessert without its special bucket-shaped **charlotte mold.** Other molds simply aim to amuse, and liven up a molded dish.

Tin is used for many of the elaborate, hand-made molds imported from Italy, Portugal and Mexico. These often have

classic geometric forms that have been used for hundreds of years, with many flat planes and pointed peaks. Typical shapes include turreted castles, craggily pointed spires, a ring-shaped, many-peaked steeple and the classic crown. The Mexicans, particularly, are more modern and let their imaginations run riot with Kewpie dolls, Mickey Mouse and blossoming daisies. The molds are hand-soldered from tin-plate, which makes them unsuitable for oven use.

Ice cream and **parfait molds** are made of similar materials. They come in less elaborate shapes, such as the favorite melon and the traditional tall cone with a rounded top.

Also of tin-plate are the small, pointed **cone molds** for shaping cream horns or ham with a mousse filling and the **high, hinged molds** for raised veal and ham or game pies. These can be round, oval or square and are often patterned to impress a low relief design on the pastry. The handsome aluminum **fish-, chicken-** and **lobster-shaped molds** are used as a kind of code identification for the contents of the mold — preparing the viewer visually for the flavor to come. Traditionally these molds were made of earthenware, and they can still be found in that material in gourmet kitchen stores.

Ring molds are universally useful and come in large or small individual serving sizes. The shallower ones are used for savory gelatins, hot and cold rice rings and for the yeast dough cake called savarin. The higher molds, called **kugelhopf** pans, are often fluted and are used for coffeecakes like kugelhopf and fruit gelatins.

Small individual molds come in myriad designs, from the classic flower-form **brioche** shape to small aluminum rabbits and fish.

Gelatin molds, for making the sparkling, jewel-like desserts that tremble so effectively at summer parties, are now generally obtainable in aluminum. They can shape high-domed, circular desserts with many-faceted peaks and sides that resemble molded glass. Other designs will produce moons and stars, hearts and flowers, clover leaves and Christmas trees, gingerbread men and pineapples — shapes to suit all seasons and every whim.

Butter molds, used simply as decorative shapes, are generally made of wood. There are two main types: the large mold, often decorated with floral reliefs into which you press a half pound or so of butter; and the small kind that produces individual pats. **Wooden molds** are also used for shaping such delicacies as shortbread, springerle

Molds shown from left to right are: peaked gelatin, charlotte with lid, fish mousse, melon, kugelhopf, ring, raised pie, conical ice cream, brioche and wooden cookie

and other firm dough cookies, that are then turned out of the molds before baking.

For successful molding, if cooking in a **tin mold,** lightly butter or oil it before adding the mixture. Wash tin molds thoroughly and dry them quickly to prevent rusting after use.

Wooden molds should be buttered and floured for cookies or thoroughly soaked in cold salt water for molding butter.

Any mold containing gelatin will release its contents easily if dipped quickly into warm water before inverting (see page 18). If the mold still sticks when inverted, carefully break the airlock by inserting the tip of a knife down the side of the mold.

Ice cream and **parfait molds** should be dipped in cold, not warm, water and inverted onto a folded white napkin to catch the drips.

Choose a mold to suit the recipe; highly peaked molds, for example, are not suitable for creamy desserts — for these, low rounded forms are less likely to collapse when unmolding.

Carve roast fillet of beef Dubarry in thick slices; garnish with tiny cauliflowers coated with mornay sauce

THANKSGIVING DINNER WITH A DIFFERENCE

If you are giving a small Thanksgiving dinner party, make a break from tradition and serve a roasted fillet of beef or pheasant in a rich, sour cream sauce for the entrée, with an easy-to-prepare appetizer and dessert.

Either of these magnificent entrées will be complemented by a fine red Burgundy of a good year. One of the most famous names of France's Côte de Beaune is Aloxe Corton and the red wines of this village will accompany this menu admirably. If you can find and afford them, you may wish to have one of the great single vineyard wines like Le Corton, Clos du Roi or Les Bressandes. A less expensive alternative, although not really in the same class, would be a well-aged Pinot Noir from a top California vineyard in the San Francisco Bay area.

Broiled Grapefruit
or
Cream of Chestnut Soup

Roast Fillet of Beef Dubarry
Château Potatoes
or
Pheasant Smetana
Boiled Rice

Strawberry Japonais

∼∾

Red wine – Aloxe Corton (Côte de Beaune)
or Pinot Noir (California)

TIMETABLE

Day before
Make chestnut soup; do not add cream.
Make and bake almond meringue for japonais and store in airtight container. Brown and grind almonds for decoration.

Morning
Prepare the grapefruit, add the sherry and place in broiling pan.
Cook the cauliflower; make mornay sauce. Press cauliflower flowerets, coat with sauce and cheese and cover.
Peel and shape château potatoes and keep in cold water.
Bard and tie fillet (if necessary).
Boil rice, drain, dry and put in dish ready for reheating.
Make coffee-flavored icing, prepare strawberries and Chantilly cream and complete japonais. Chill.

Assemble equipment for final cooking from 3 p.m. for dinner around 5 p.m.

Order of Work
3:00
Set oven at hot (400°F) *or* moderate (350°F).
3:20
Heat the oil in a roasting pan, baste beef and roast in heated oven.
3:50
Baste beef.
Brown the pheasants, add the shallot and wine, cover and bake in heated oven or simmer on top of stove (put smaller birds in at 4 p.m.).
Brown the potatoes in butter, drain and cover.

4:00
Put the potatoes on lower oven shelf.
4:15
Remove the potatoes; baste beef *or turn the pheasants.*
4:25
Transfer meat to lower shelf and put cauliflower on upper shelf.
4:30
Turn the pheasants.
4:40
Take the beef and cauliflower from oven. Turn heat to broil for the grapefruit.
Arrange the beef with the cauliflower on a platter and keep warm.
Make the gravy.
Remove the pheasants and keep warm; make sauce. Reheat rice in oven.
4:50
Add the butter and sugar to grapefruit and broil.
Reheat soup; add cream.
Reheat the potatoes.
Carve the pheasants, arrange on a platter and keep warm.
5:00
Serve appetizer.
Transfer potatoes to a dish just before serving.
Add sour cream to sauce and spoon over pheasants just before serving.

You will find that **cooking times** given in the individual recipes for these dishes have sometimes been adapted in the timetable to help you when cooking and serving this menu as a party meal.

Appetizer

Broiled Grapefruit

3–4 grapefruit
3–4 tablespoons sherry
3–4 tablespoons dark brown sugar
2 tablespoons butter

When choosing grapefruit, look for well-shaped ones that are heavy for their size. They should feel firm and springy — avoid those with softened or pointed ends and a puffy appearance.

Method
To prepare grapefruit: using a grapefruit knife (with a curved serrated edge), remove the core, then cut around the edge of the grapefruit between the flesh and the pith so the flesh is completely detached from the shell. Slip the knife down each side of the membrane dividing the grapefruit sections, then lift out all the membranes in one piece. Remove any seeds.

For broiled grapefruit, sprinkle each grapefruit half with about 1 tablespoon sherry and set in a broiler pan. This can be done several hours before.

Just before serving, heat the broiler, sprinkle sugar over the grapefruit and dot with butter. Broil 5–6 minutes or until the sugar is lightly caramelized but not burned. Serve hot.

Before broiling grapefruit, remove core, cut the flesh away from pith and separate the sections

Broiled grapefruit, with lightly caramelized tops, take only a few minutes to cook

Note: all recipes on pages 34–39 serve 6–8 people.

Cream of Chestnut Soup

2 lb fresh chestnuts, skinned
4 cups chicken or veal stock
$\frac{1}{2}$ cup butter
2 medium onions, finely
   chopped
6 stalks of celery, chopped
salt and pepper
kneaded butter (made with
   2 tablespoons butter and
   1 tablespoon flour) — optional
1 cup light cream

For croûtons
4 slices of bread
2 tablespoons oil (for frying)
$\frac{1}{4}$ cup butter (for frying)

Method

Put the skinned chestnuts in a pan with enough of the stock to cover and $\frac{1}{4}$ cup of the butter. Cover and cook over low heat for 30 minutes or until very soft. Work through a sieve or food mill or purée in a blender.

Melt the remaining butter in a large pan, add the onion, cover and cook until soft but not brown. Stir in the chestnut purée; then add the remaining stock and celery. Season to taste, bring to a boil, stirring, and simmer 20 minutes. Fry the croûtons, drain and keep hot.

If necessary, whisk a little kneaded butter into the hot soup to thicken it. Strain the soup, add the cream, bring just back to a boil and taste again for seasoning. Serve with the croûtons in a separate bowl.

Cream of chestnut soup is garnished with a few croûtons

Entrée

Roast Fillet of Beef Dubarry

4–5 lb fillet (tenderloin) of beef
thinly sliced pork fat
  (for barding)
2–3 tablespoons oil or beef
  drippings

For garnish
1 large or 2 medium
  cauliflowers
$\frac{1}{4}$ cup grated Cheddar cheese

For thick mornay sauce
$\frac{1}{4}$ cup butter
$\frac{1}{4}$ cup flour
2 cups milk
$\frac{3}{4}$ cup grated Parmesan or dry
  Cheddar cheese
salt and pepper

For gravy
1 tablespoon flour
$1\frac{1}{2}$–2 cups beef stock

Method
To prepare the garnish: break
the cauliflower into flowerets
and cook in boiling salted
water for 5–7 minutes or until
just tender. Drain and refresh
under cold water.

Place 1–2 flowerets in a
square of cheesecloth and
fold, twisting the cloth so the
cauliflower forms a ball.
Unwrap the cloth and set the
ball on a buttered baking
sheet. Continue until all the
cauliflower is used, making
about 12 miniature cauli-
flowers.

Make the mornay sauce
and coat the cauliflowers with
it. Sprinkle with grated
cheese, cover with plastic
wrap and reserve. This garnish
can be prepared 4 – 6 hours
ahead.

Set oven at hot (400°F). If

the butcher has not already
done so, wrap the fillet of beef
in pork fat and tie in a neat
cylinder with string.

Heat the oil or drippings
in a roasting pan, baste the
beef, place it on a rack in the
pan and roast in heated oven,
basting often, allowing 15
minutes per lb for rare meat
(140°F) on a meat ther-
mometer).

Take the meat from the
oven, transfer it to a carving
board and keep warm. Bake
the cauliflowers in heated
oven for 10–15 minutes or
until brown.

To make the gravy: pour
the fat from the pan and
discard it, leaving the sediment. Stir the flour into the
pan and cook over medium
heat, stirring, until the flour is
brown. Add the stock, bring
to a boil and simmer until the
gravy is well reduced, stirring
to dissolve any sediment.
Taste for seasoning and strain.

Carve the meat in thick
slices and arrange on a warm
platter with the cauliflower
garnish around the edge.
Spoon a little gravy over the
beef and serve the rest separately. Serve with château
potatoes.

*To prepare the garnish for
fillet of beef Dubarry: press
1–2 flowerets of cooked
cauliflower in a piece of
cheesecloth and fold and
twist to form miniature cauli-*

Château Potatoes

20–24 small new potatoes
  or 6 medium white potatoes
6–8 tablespoons butter
salt

Method
If using white potatoes, peel
them, cut in quarters lengthwise and trim off the sharp
edges with a vegetable
peeler. Blanch them by putting them in cold water and
bringing to a boil, then drain.
If using new potatoes, scrub
them with a pot scrubber or
small brush to remove skin
(or use a vegetable peeler).

In a flameproof casserole
melt the butter, add the
potatoes and cook over
moderate heat until golden
brown all over, occasionally
shaking to turn them and
prevent them from sticking.
Sprinkle lightly with salt,
cover and bake in a hot oven
(400°F) for 10–12 minutes or
until tender.

*flowers. Place these miniature
cauliflowers on a buttered
baking sheet, coat them with
thick mornay sauce and
sprinkle with cheese before
browning in the oven*

Pheasant Smetana

2–3 plump pheasants
6 tablespoons butter
salt and pepper
4 shallots, chopped
1 cup white wine

For sauce
6 shallots, finely chopped
$1\frac{1}{2}$ cups white wine
1 tablespoon flour
2 cups sour cream

Trussing needle and string

Method
Wipe the birds inside and out
with a damp cloth or paper
towel. Put 1 tablespoon
butter, mixed with salt and
pepper, inside each pheasant
and truss.

Heat remaining butter in a
flameproof casserole and
brown the pheasants on all
sides over medium heat. Add
the shallots, wine and seasoning, cover pot and simmer on
top of the stove or bake in a
moderate oven (350°F) for
40–50 minutes for large
birds, 35–40 minutes for
smaller ones, or until tender,
turning birds from time to
time. Pour the cooking liquid
from the pot and reserve, but
leave the birds in the pot,
covered.

To prepare the sauce:
simmer the shallots in the
wine in a saucepan until the
wine is reduced by half, then
let stand. Skim fat from the
reserved cooking liquid, put
fat in another saucepan and
stir in the flour. Strain in the
cooking liquid, add the
reduced wine and shallots

and bring to a boil, stirring. Simmer 2 minutes and take from the heat.

Carve the pheasants and arrange on a platter. Stir the sour cream into the sauce, reheat without boiling, taste for seasoning and strain over the pheasants. Serve with boiled rice.

Pheasant smetana is cooked in white wine with sour cream and shallots. The name 'smetana' comes from the Russian word for sour cream

Dessert

Strawberry Japonais

1 quart fresh strawberries or
  2 packages frozen
  strawberries
1½ cups whole almonds,
  blanched and ground
1½ cups sugar
6 egg whites
little granulated sugar
  (for sprinkling)
1 cup milk icing or glacé icing,
  flavored with 2 teaspoons
  dry instant coffee
1 cup Chantilly cream, made
  with ½ cup heavy cream,
  3–4 teaspoons sugar,
  ½ teaspoon vanilla
½ cup blanched almonds
  (for decoration) – optional

A japonais is made of
meringue and ground almonds
or pistachios. It can be baked
and sandwiched with a variety
of fillings.

Method
Set oven at low (300°F). Line
2 baking sheets with silicone
paper and mark a 9 inch circle
on each.

To make the japonais: mix
the ground almonds with the
sugar and sift through a coarse
strainer to blend thoroughly.
Beat the egg whites until they
hold a stiff peak, then fold in
the almond and sugar mixture,
half at a time. Spread this
mixture into two 9 inch rounds
on the prepared baking sheets
and bake in heated oven for
about 1 hour or until lightly
browned. Lift the japonais
rounds carefully onto a rack
and, when cool but not cold,
peel off the paper.

Brown the whole almonds
in a moderate oven (350°F)
for 7–8 minutes, cool and

grind them in a rotary nut
grater.

If using fresh strawberries,
reserve a few for decoration,
halve the rest and sprinkle
with a little sugar. If using
frozen ones, thaw and drain
thoroughly.

Pour the coffee-flavored
icing over one japonais round
to coat it completely. Spoon
the Chantilly cream onto the
other round and top with the
halved fresh strawberries or
the frozen ones. Place the
iced round on top of this
filling and press the ground
browned almonds around the
sides. Decorate the top with
whole fresh strawberries or
leave plain if using frozen
strawberries or decorate with
halved blanched almonds, if
you like.

*Completely cover one japonais
meringue round with the
coffee-flavored icing*

*Cover the japonais base with
Chantilly cream and spoon
on the strawberries; place the
iced round on top and decorate*

Glacé Icing

To make 1½ cups: in a pan
dissolve ¼ cup sugar in
½ cup water over low heat,
bring to a boil and simmer
4–5 minutes. Take pan
from heat and when cold
beat 2 cups confectioners'
sugar into sugar syrup, 1
tablespoon at a time.

Set pan over another
pan of hot water and
warm until lukewarm; the
icing should coat the back
of a spoon but still pour
easily. Add more confec-
tioners' sugar (about 1
tablespoon) or a little extra
sugar syrup until it is the
right consistency.

Milk Icing

To make 1 cup: melt 1
teaspoon butter in a
saucepan, add 1½ cups
sugar and ½ cup milk and
cook, stirring, until the
mixture comes to a boil.
Boil, without stirring, until
a long thread forms when
syrup is tested between
fingers and thumb (234°F
on a sugar thermometer).
Cool, then beat until the
icing reaches a spreading
consistency.
Watchpoint: if the icing
hardens before you can
use it, place the pan over
hot water, melt icing and
beat it a second time;
this usually ensures that
the icing will stay the right
consistency.

Strawberry japonais, sandwiched with Chantilly cream, is decorated with icing and whole strawberries

French roast turkey, garnished with watercress and crispy bacon, is traditional fare for Thanksgiving

THANKSGIVING DAY IDEAS

Choose a festive menu for Thanksgiving dinner from the array of appetizers, entrées, accompaniments, and desserts that we suggest — almost any combination will be excellent but try to avoid repeating a distinctive flavor like apple.

Then look at the timetable on page 43 to help you prepare part of your dinner in advance. All recipes listed are included in this Volume and all appetizers, accompaniments and desserts serve 6–8 people.

APPETIZER	**Cold**: Avocado in Tarragon Cream Dressing or Grapefruit and Grape Salad		
	Hot: Cream of Corn Soup		

ENTREE	**Turkey (French roast)**	**Capon (roast)**	**Goose (roast)**
	Pork or Veal Stuffing, or Celery, Apricot and Pecan Stuffing	Pork or Veal Stuffing, or Celery, Apricot and Pecan Stuffing	Potato and Apple Stuffing, or Apple, Pecan and Prune Stuffing, or Brazilian Stuffing
	Chestnut Stuffing or Wild Rice Stuffing	Chestnut Stuffing or Wild Rice Stuffing	Spiced Apples or Apple Sauce
	Cranberry Sauce	Cranberry Sauce	Braised Red Cabbage
	Glazed Sweet Potatoes	Duchesse Potatoes	Buttered Turnips
	Scalloped Oysters	Glazed Onions with Chestnuts	Baked Acorn Squash
	Braised Celery	Crisp Bacon	
	Onions in Cream	Chipolata Sausages	

DESSERT	Pumpkin Pie, Apple Florentine, Rum Pie or Pecan Pie

TIMETABLE

APPETIZERS

Avocado in Tarragon Cream Dressing: prepare the dressing 1–2 days before but add the cream just before using, cover and chill; halve the avocados, remove the seeds and coat with dressing 15–30 minutes before serving.
Grapefruit and Grape Salad: prepare the grapefruit (see page 34), grapes and dressing the day before and refrigerate; spoon over the dressing just before serving.
Cream of Corn Soup: prepare the day before, cover and refrigerate; reheat before serving.
Choux or Cheese Puffs: make them the day before and store in an airtight container.

ENTREES

Roast Turkey: stuff, truss and cook in morning.
Roast Capon: stuff, truss and cook in morning.
Roast Goose: stuff, truss and cook in morning.

STUFFINGS

Apple, Pecan and Prune: make 1–2 days before, cover and refrigerate.
Brazilian: make the day before, cover and refrigerate.
Celery, Apricot and Pecan: prepare 1–2 days before, cover and refrigerate.
Chestnut: make 1–2 days before, cover and refrigerate.
Pork or Veal: make in the morning, cover and refrigerate.
Potato and Apple: make the day before, cover and refrigerate but do not add the apples; pare, core and chop the apples and add to the stuffing just before using.
Wild Rice: make the day before, cover and refrigerate.

ACCOMPANIMENTS

Apple Sauce: prepare 1–2 days before; reheat before serving.
Bacon: in the morning fry or broil until crisp; drain; reheat before serving.
Baked Acorn Squash: prepare and bake until tender the day before and cover; finish with sugar and reheat before serving.
Braised Celery: braise the day before until tender; reheat just before serving.
Braised Red Cabbage: cook the day before; reheat just before serving.
Buttered Turnips: boil and mash 30 minutes before dinner; keep warm with hot half and half.
Chipolata Sausages: in the morning simmer them in water and drain; reheat by frying.
Cranberry Sauce: make 1–2 days before; serve cold.
Duchesse Potatoes: make the day before or in the morning and leave piped on a baking sheet, covered; bake just before serving.
Glazed Onions and Chestnuts: simmer the skinned chestnuts and blanch and glaze the onions the day before; reheat together before serving.
Onions in Cream: cook until tender and arrange in a covered serving dish the day before; reheat the onions, make the sauce and pour over the onions just before serving.
Glazed Sweet Potatoes: cook and arrange them in a baking dish the day before or in the morning and cover; bake before serving.
Scalloped Oysters: prepare in the morning; bake before serving.
Spiced Apples: prepare and bake 15–30 minutes in the morning; finish baking until tender before serving.

PIES

Apple Florentine, Pecan and Pumpkin Pies: make the day before; reheat before serving or serve cold.
Rum Pie: bake the pie shell the day before and add the filling in the morning; add the topping 1–2 hours before serving.

Note: all pastry may be prepared 1–2 days before and stored in a plastic bag in refrigerator.

Avocado in Tarragon Cream Dressing

3—4 avocados
6—12 Bibb or Boston lettuce
    leaves
paprika (for sprinkling)

For tarragon cream dressing
$\frac{1}{4}$ cup tarragon vinegar
1 cup heavy cream, whipped
    until it holds a soft shape
$\frac{1}{2}$ teaspoon sugar (or to taste)
2 small eggs, beaten to mix
salt and pepper

This quantity makes enough dressing to coat 6—8 avocado halves.

Method
To prepare the dressing: add the sugar to the eggs in a bowl and gradually pour in the vinegar. Stand the bowl in a pan of boiling water and stir until the mixture begins to thicken, then remove from the heat and continue stirring. When the mixture is thick, take the bowl out of the pan and stir 1 minute longer; season lightly and cool. Fold the cream into dressing.

Arrange 1—2 lettuce leaves on individual plates. Halve, seed and peel the avocados. Arrange the halves on the plates, rounded side up, coat with the dressing, sprinkle with paprika and serve.

Note: all recipes on pages 44—53 serve 6—8 people.

For an unusual appetizer try avocado in tarragon cream dressing or a refreshing grapefruit and grape salad

Grapefruit and Grape Salad

3 large grapefruits
$\frac{1}{2}$ lb green grapes
1—2 tablespoons sugar

For dressing
$\frac{1}{4}$ cup oil
2 tablespoons lemon juice
$\frac{1}{2}$ teaspoon sugar (or to taste)
salt
black pepper, freshly ground
2 teaspoons chopped mint or
    parsley

Method
Cut the grapefruits in half, remove the cores and cut around the edges of the grapefruits between the flesh and the white pith with a grapefruit knife to detach the flesh from the shells. Slip the knife carefully down each side of the pieces of membrane to separate the sections and lift out all the membranes in one piece.

If possible use seedless grapes, but if these are not available scoop out the seeds with the end of a bobby pin, sterilized in a flame. Pile a few grapes in the center of each grapefruit half, sprinkle with sugar and chill.

To make the dressing: mix the oil and lemon juice, whisk well and add the sugar and seasoning to taste with mint or parsley. Pour a tablespoon of dressing over each grapefruit before serving.

Cream of Corn Soup

1 cup canned or fresh creamed
    corn
1 cup cooked frozen or fresh
    whole corn kernels or 1 cup
    canned, drained corn
    kernels (optional)
3 tablespoons butter
2 medium potatoes,
    finely sliced
1 medium onion, finely sliced
1 tablespoon flour
$2\frac{1}{2}$ cups milk
$1\frac{1}{2}$ cups water
1 bay leaf
salt and pepper
choux or cheese puffs
    (for garnish) — optional

Whole corn kernels will give this soup body, but they are not essential.

Method
In a kettle melt the butter, add the potatoes and onion, cover and cook very gently for 5—7 minutes or until the vegetables are soft but not browned. Stir in the flour and add the milk, water, bay leaf and seasoning. Bring to a boil, stirring well. Add the creamed corn and simmer gently for 15—20 minutes. Remove bay leaf.

Purée the soup in a blender or work it through a sieve or food mill. Return it to the kettle with the whole corn kernels, if used, reheat the soup and adjust seasoning. Serve with choux or cheese puffs.

Choux Puffs

Make a small quantity of choux pastry in the following proportions (be sure to measure accurately): $\frac{1}{2}$ cup flour, pinch of salt, $\frac{1}{2}$ cup water, $\frac{1}{4}$ cup butter and 2 eggs (see Volume 6 for how to make choux pastry).

Spoon the pastry dough into a pastry bag fitted with a $\frac{1}{4}$ inch plain tube and pipe tiny mounds on a dampened baking sheet. Bake in a hot oven (400°F) for 12–15 minutes or until the puffs are brown and crisp. Cool before serving. This quantity makes enough puffs for 6–8 people.

Cheese Puffs

Follow the recipe for choux puffs and add $\frac{1}{4}$ cup grated Parmesan cheese to the dough before piping.

ENTREES

Turkey

Today's turkeys come in many sizes and types including butterball turkeys bred especially for their plump breast meat. Many turkeys are frozen and should be thoroughly thawed — preferably in the refrigerator — before cooking. Allow 24 hours in the refrigerator for every 6 lb of turkey or, if thawing at room temperature, allow 1 hour per lb.

Turkeys, particularly if they are large, tend to dry out during cooking and French roasting with stock and plenty of butter helps to prevent this. An alternative is to wrap them in foil and slow roast them — this gives a moist tender bird but some cooks feel that the turkey steams in its own juice rather than roasts and there are fewer pan juices for making gravy.

To test if the bird is done, insert a skewer in the thickest part of the thigh — the juice that runs out should be clear and not pink. The most reliable test is a meat thermometer, which should register 185°F when inserted into the center of the inside of the thigh but not touching the bone.

Turkeys that have been specially prepared — birds frozen with stuffing inside, for example — should be cooked according to package directions.

Allow 1 lb turkey per person — a 10 lb turkey will serve 10 people.

To Slow Roast a Turkey

Set oven at moderately low (325°F).

Rub the turkey all over with $\frac{3}{4}$–1 cup butter (depending on size); wrap in foil, place it in a roasting pan and roast in heated oven, allowing 20 minutes per lb and 30 minutes extra for birds 14 lb and under; for birds over 14 lb, allow 18 minutes per lb and 15 minutes extra.

Unwrap the bird about 35 minutes before the end of roasting so it can brown, and pour the juice in the foil into the pan — this will help to make the gravy, although it will not be as brown as with regular roasting.

If the bird shows no sign of browning, turn oven heat to hot (400°F) 15 minutes before the end of roasting.

COOKING TIMES FOR POULTRY

(at 185°F on Meat Thermometer)	Quantities for Serving (per person)	Cooking Times	Oven Temperature
Turkey			
(under 10 lb)	1 lb	20 minutes per lb plus 20 minutes more	350°F
(10–14 lb)	1 lb	18 minutes per lb	350°F
(over 14 lb)	1 lb	16 minutes per lb	350°F
Capon	1 lb	25 minutes per lb	375°F
Goose	$1\frac{1}{4}$–$1\frac{1}{2}$ lb	18 minutes per lb	375°F–350°F

Note: weigh bird before stuffing. If bird is to be cooked without stuffing, allow 15–45 minutes less cooking time, depending on size.

French Roast Turkey

1 turkey
pork or veal stuffing or celery, apricot and pecan stuffing (for carcass)
chestnut stuffing or wild rice stuffing (for breast)
2–2½ cups stock (made from giblets – except liver – 1 sliced onion, 1 sliced carrot, few peppercorns, little salt, bouquet garni)
¾–1 cup butter (depending on size of bird)
1 tablespoon flour (to thicken gravy)
salt and pepper
bunch of watercress (for garnish)

Trussing needle; string or skewer

Method

Set oven at moderate (350°F).

Prepare the stuffing (see pages 48–49). Put the pork or veal stuffing or celery, apricot and pecan stuffing through the vent end of the bird. Draw the thighs close to the body and fasten to the pope's nose with string. Loosen the neck skin and fill the breast cavity well with the chestnut or wild rice stuffing, mounding it under the skin. Pull the skin gently over the stuffing and fasten it under the wing tips. Sew with string or fasten with a skewer.

Put the turkey in a roasting pan and pour around half the stock. Thickly butter a sheet of foil and lay over the bird, tucking in the edges slightly without sealing. Roast in heated oven for the time indicated in the chart on page 45 or until the bird tests done.

Turn and baste the bird every 20 minutes and keep the foil on top throughout roasting. If the bird is not browned enough near the end of roasting, remove the foil. If the stock reduces too much, add a little more. After 1–2 hours (depending on the size of the bird), loosen the string holding the legs to let the heat reach the inside of the thighs.

When cooked, transfer the turkey to a platter, pull out the trussing strings and skewer and keep turkey warm.

To make the gravy: strain the juices from the roasting pan into a saucepan and dissolve the pan sediment in the remaining stock. Add this to the saucepan, skim off any fat and return fat to the roasting pan. Stir in the flour, then pour in the juices from the saucepan. Bring the gravy to a boil, stirring, and simmer 2 minutes. Strain back into the saucepan and taste for seasoning. Heat thoroughly and serve separately.

Garnish the turkey with a bunch of watercress just before serving. Carve at the table.

Note: all recipes on pages 44–53 serve 6–8 people.

To Carve a Turkey

Set the bird on a carving board or platter with the breast towards you. Insert the fork into the carcass between the leg and breast, then slice the skin between the leg and carcass; bend the leg out. Carve the breast in slanting slices, parallel to the rib cage, starting at the wing end and working towards the pope's nose. Include some of the stuffing with each slice

Cut the drumstick from the thigh and on a large turkey cut thin slices of dark meat, parallel to the bone, from both the drumstick and thigh. If the turkey is small, simply cut the legs in half at the joint. When one side of the bird is carved, turn it around and carve the other side

Capon

Capon is an excellent alternative to turkey for a small dinner. These neutered cock chickens are luxuriously plump and white with a delicate flavor. They weigh from 5 lb (which serves 5 people) up to 12 lb, serving 12 people.

Capon can be French roasted like turkey or oven roasted as below, when crisp bacon and chipolata sausages are a good garnish. Depending on its size, the bird should be stuffed with one or two of the stuffings suggested for turkey.

Roast Capon

1 capon
pork or veal stuffing or celery, apricot and pecan stuffing (for carcass)
chestnut stuffing or wild rice stuffing (for breast)
3–4 tablespoons butter
1 tablespoon flour (to thicken gravy)
1½ cups stock (made with giblets – except liver – 1 sliced onion, 1 sliced carrot, few peppercorns, little salt, bouquet garni)
salt and pepper

For garnish
½ lb sliced bacon
½ lb chipolata sausages
bunch of watercress

Trussing needle; string or skewer

Method

Set oven at moderately hot (375°F).

Prepare the stuffings (see pages 48—49) and put the pork or veal stuffing through the vent end of the bird. Draw the thighs close to the body and fasten to the pope's nose with string.

Loosen the neck skin and fill the breast cavity well with the chestnut or wild rice stuffing, mounding it under the skin. Pull the skin gently over the stuffing and fasten it under the wing tips. Sew with string or fasten with a skewer. If using only one stuffing, fill the bird from the vent end.

Melt the butter in a roasting pan, put in the capon and baste it. Roast in heated oven for the time indicated in the chart on page 45 or until the bird tests done. Turn and baste every 20 minutes.

To test if the bird is done, insert a skewer in the thickest part of the thigh — the juice that runs out should be clear and not pink. The most reliable test is a meat thermometer which should register 185°F when inserted into the center of the inside of the thigh but not touching the bone.

When the capon is almost cooked, prepare the garnishes. Broil or fry the bacon until crisp, drain on paper towels and keep warm. Simmer the chipolata sausages in water to cover for 8—10 minutes, then fry them gently until they are brown, drain and keep warm.

When cooked, transfer the capon to a platter and pull out the trussing strings and skewer; keep the capon warm.

To make the gravy: pour off all but 1—2 tablespoons fat from the roasting pan and discard. Stir the flour into the pan, pour in the stock and bring to a boil, stirring and scraping to dissolve the sediment. Simmer 2—3 minutes, strain into a saucepan, reheat

and taste for seasoning.

Arrange the bacon and sausages around the capon, add a bunch of watercress and serve the gravy separately. Carve a capon like a turkey.

Goose

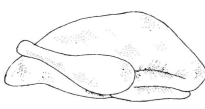

The rich dark meat of goose is splendid fare for feasting. Unfortunately goose has been eclipsed by turkey and is generally available only through special poultry shops, although most supermarkets carry frozen geese for Thanksgiving.

Goose is much more like duck than chicken or turkey and tart fruit flavors best complement its richness. Stuffings should include some ingredient like potato or rice to absorb fat from the meat. During cooking be sure that the fat from under the skin is drained adequately.

Goose is not economical because it is a bony bird and you will need $1\frac{1}{4}$—$1\frac{1}{2}$ lb per person.

Roast Goose

1 goose
apple and potato stuffing, or apple, pecan and prune stuffing, or Brazilian stuffing
salt and pepper
2—3 tablespoons cold water
2—3 teaspoons flour (to thicken gravy)
$1\frac{1}{2}$ cups stock (made from giblets — except liver — 1 sliced onion, 1 sliced carrot, few peppercorns, little salt, bouquet garni)

Trussing needle; string or skewer

Method

Set oven at moderately hot (375°F).

Prepare the stuffing (see pages 48—49). Rub inside the bird with salt and pepper and put the stuffing through the vent end. Draw the thighs close to the body and fasten to the pope's nose with string. Fold neck skin under the bird, bend it under the wing tips and sew with string and a trussing needle or fasten with a skewer.

Sprinkle the bird with salt and pepper and place on a rack in a roasting pan. Prick the skin to release the fat and roast in a heated oven for the time indicated in the chart on page 45 or until the bird tests done. Halfway through roasting, lower heat to moderate (350°F). Turn and baste the bird every 20 minutes.

Ten minutes before the end of roasting, set the bird on its back and pour the cold water over the breast — this makes the skin crisp.

To test if the bird is done, insert a skewer in the thickest part of the thigh — the juice that runs out should be clear and not pink. The most reliable test is a meat thermometer, which should

register 185°F when inserted into the center of the inside of the thigh but not touching the bone.

When cooked, transfer the goose to a platter and pull out the trussing strings and skewer and keep it warm.

To make the gravy: pour off all but 1—2 tablespoons fat from the roasting pan and discard. Stir the flour into the pan, pour in the stock and bring to a boil, stirring and scraping to dissolve the sediment. Simmer 2—3 minutes and strain into a saucepan. Reheat, taste for seasoning and serve separately.

To carve roast goose: set the bird on a carving board and cut off the legs, remembering that the joints are set under the back. Cut the legs in half through the thigh joint and slice the meat from the bone if the bird is large. Slip a knife between the breastbone and breast to loosen the meat. Sever the wing joint, angling the knife so that a good piece of the breast meat is left attached to each wing.

To slice the breast, make a series of cuts parallel to the breastbone, slanting the knife towards the inside of the bird. (See diagrams of carving a goose in Volume 1.)

STUFFINGS

Stuffing adds flavor to a bird, particularly when the meat tends to be bland as it can be with turkey and capon. For large birds it is worth making two stuffings of contrasting flavor and texture, putting them at each end of the bird.

Be sure a stuffing is cool before filling the bird and cook the bird within 2–3 hours. (See quantity guide chart right.)

Note: all recipes on pages 44–53 serve 6–8 people.

STUFFING QUANTITY GUIDE

Size of Bird	Amount of Stuffing
6 lb	3–4 cups
8 lb	5–6 cups
10 lb	7–8 cups
14 lb	10–12 cups
18 lb	13–15 cups
24 lb	18–20 cups

Turkey can be stuffed with a variety of ingredients like ground veal, breadcrumbs, celery, onion and herbs, apricots and pecans

Stuffings for Turkey and Capon

Pork or Veal Stuffing

1½ lb sausage meat or ¾ lb sausage meat and ¾ lb ground pork or veal (mixed)
3 tablespoons butter
1 large onion, finely chopped
1 tablespoon chopped parsley
½ teaspoon thyme
½ teaspoon sage
1 cup fresh white breadcrumbs
salt and pepper
1 egg, beaten to mix
little stock (taken from stock for gravy)

Makes about 4 cups.

Method
Melt the butter in a pan, add the onion, cover and cook until soft. Add to the meat with the herbs and bread-crumbs and plenty of salt and pepper. Mix thoroughly, then add the egg and enough stock to bind the mixture. Refrigerate until needed.

Celery, Apricot and Pecan Stuffing

small bunch of celery, thinly sliced
½ cup dried apricots
1 cup chopped pecans
3 tablespoons butter
2 onions, chopped
1½ cups fresh white breadcrumbs
1 tablespoon chopped parsley
salt and pepper

Makes about 5 cups.

Method
Soak the apricots, if necessary, according to the package directions. Drain them and cut each half in 3–4 pieces.

Melt the butter in a pan, add the onion, cover and cook until soft. Add the celery, apricots and pecans and cook 3–4 minutes over medium heat, stirring constantly. Transfer to a bowl and cool. Stir in the breadcrumbs and parsley and season to taste.

Chestnut Stuffing

1 lb fresh chestnuts, skinned (see box)
1–1½ cups stock
2 cups fresh white breadcrumbs
1 onion, finely chopped
2 tablespoons melted butter
1 teaspoon thyme
salt and pepper
2 eggs, beaten to mix

Makes about 4 cups.

Method
Put the chestnuts in a pan with stock to cover and cover with the lid. Simmer 30–40 minutes or until tender. Drain the chestnuts and work them through a sieve or purée in a

blender with a little of the stock.

Stir in the breadcrumbs, onion, melted butter, thyme and season to taste. Beat in enough egg to make a mixture that falls from a spoon but is not too soupy.

To skin fresh chestnuts: prick the shells with the point of a knife. Put the nuts in a pan of cold water, bring to a boil, then take from the heat and peel them while they are still hot, taking off the outer and inner skins.

Wild Rice Stuffing

1 cup wild rice
4 cups chicken stock
2 tablespoons butter
2 shallots or scallions, finely chopped
1 cup ($\frac{1}{4}$ lb) sliced mushrooms
juice of $\frac{1}{2}$ lemon
salt and pepper

Makes about 4 cups.

Method
Simmer the rice, covered, with the stock for 40–45 minutes or until all the stock is absorbed and the rice is tender. If the rice is cooked before all the stock is absorbed, uncover the pan and boil until the liquid has evaporated.

In a small pan melt the butter and sauté the shallots or scallions until soft. Add the mushrooms and cook over medium heat for 2–3 minutes or until all the moisture has evaporated. Add the lemon juice, stir the mushroom mixture into the rice and season to taste.

To Stuff a Turkey

Above: first stuff body cavity of bird through vent end (be sure stuffing is cool)
Below: draw the thighs close to the body and tie string around the knuckle joints and pope's nose

Above: to stuff neck end, fill breast cavity, mounding the stuffing well; fold the skin over the stuffing and tuck under the wing tips
Below: sew up the neck end of the bird to keep stuffing in place or fasten securely with a skewer

Stuffings for Goose

Brazilian Stuffing

3 tablespoons olive oil
2 medium onions, chopped
1 green pepper, cored, seeded and chopped
$\frac{1}{2}$ lb ground pork
1 cup whole blanched almonds, ground
$\frac{1}{2}$ cup raisins
2 hard-cooked eggs, chopped
$\frac{1}{2}$ cup pimiento-stuffed green olives, sliced
3 slices of bread, crusts removed and diced
1 teaspoon thyme
1 tablespoon chopped parsley
salt and pepper

Makes 5–6 cups.

Method
Heat the oil and cook the onion until soft but not brown. Add the green pepper and cook until soft. Stir in the pork and cook until brown. Stir in the remaining ingredients and season well with salt and pepper to taste.

Potato and Apple Stuffing

1 lb potatoes, peeled
2 tart apples
2 medium onions, finely chopped
1 teaspoon chopped parsley
$\frac{1}{2}$ teaspoon thyme
$\frac{1}{2}$ teaspoon sage or marjoram
2 tablespoons melted butter
salt and pepper

Makes 5–6 cups.

Method
Put the potatoes in cold salted

water, bring to a boil and simmer 15–20 minutes or until just tender, then drain.

Put the onions in a pan of cold water, bring to a boil and simmer 5–7 minutes or until tender, then drain.

Pare, core and chop the apples and put in a bowl with the herbs. Dice the potatoes. Add the onions to the apple mixture with the potatoes and melted butter and stir well. Season to taste.

Apple, Pecan and Prune Stuffing

1 cup dried apple rings
1 cup chopped pecans
1 cup prunes, pitted
4 slices of bread, crusts removed and diced
1 egg, beaten to mix
3–4 tablespoons melted butter
salt and pepper

Makes about 4 cups.

Method
Pour boiling water over the apple rings and prunes and leave to soak for 15 minutes. Drain and chop them coarsely. Add the pecans and bread cubes and stir well.

Mix in the beaten egg with enough melted butter to bind the mixture and season to taste.

ACCOMPANIMENTS

Half the fun of a holiday bird is its accompaniments. They provide a welcome contrast of texture and color and should complement the flavor of the meat as well. Some accompaniments, like cranberry sauce for turkey and apple sauce with goose, are traditional, but others, like braised celery or glazed onions with chestnuts, strike a fresh note. The choice is up to you. Several of these recipes have already been given but are repeated for convenience.

Apple Sauce

1 lb tart apples, pared, cored and sliced
thinly peeled rind of $\frac{1}{2}$ lemon
2–3 tablespoons water
1 tablespoon butter
1 tablespoon sugar (or to taste)

Method
Put the apples in a saucepan with the lemon rind and water. Cover tightly and cook over low heat for 8–10 minutes or until apples are pulpy, stirring occasionally.

Remove the lemon rind and beat the apples with a wooden spoon until smooth or purée them in a blender or work them through a sieve. Stir in the butter and sugar and serve hot.

Cranberry Sauce

4 cups (1 lb) fresh cranberries
1 cup sugar (or to taste)
1 cup water
1 tablespoon port (optional)

Makes about 3 cups.

Method
Wash and pick over the cranberries. Dissolve the sugar in the water, bring to a boil and simmer 2 minutes over low heat. Add the cranberries and simmer, uncovered, for 5 minutes or until the cranberries are just tender. Take from the heat and add the port, if used, and more sugar to taste.

If you prefer a pulpy sauce, cook the cranberries 1–2 minutes longer, then crush them lightly with a wooden spoon to break them up. Cover and leave in the refrigerator until needed.

Duchesse Potatoes

mashed potatoes (made with 7–8 medium potatoes, 1 cup milk, 5–6 tablespoons butter, seasoning)
2–3 egg yolks
1 egg, beaten with $\frac{1}{2}$ teaspoon salt (for glaze)

Pastry bag and large star tube

Method
Beat the egg yolks into the hot mashed potatoes and spoon into the pastry bag fitted with the large star tube. Pipe large rosettes, figure eights or mounds of potato onto a buttered baking sheet. Brush with glaze.

Just before serving, bake potatoes in a hot oven (400°F) 8–10 minutes or until browned, or warm in a low oven, then brown quickly under the broiler.

Glazed Sweet Potatoes

6–8 sweet potatoes, peeled
1 tablespoon lemon juice
$\frac{1}{2}$ cup honey
salt and pepper
$\frac{1}{2}$ cup coarsely chopped pecans or walnuts
2 tablespoons butter

Method
Cook the potatoes in boiling salted water for 20–25 minutes or until tender. Drain, slice and arrange them, overlapping, in a buttered baking dish.

Spoon over the lemon juice and honey, sprinkle with salt, pepper and nuts and dot with butter. Bake in a moderately hot oven (375°F) for 15 minutes or until lightly browned.

Spiced Apples

8–12 small or 6–8 medium tart apples
$\frac{1}{2}$ cup honey
$\frac{1}{4}$ cup butter
$\frac{1}{2}$ teaspoon ground cinnamon
$\frac{1}{2}$ teaspoon ground allspice
$\frac{1}{4}$ teaspoon ground cloves
$\frac{1}{4}$ teaspoon ground nutmeg

Method
Wipe the apples, core them and mark a circle around the skin with a knife so they do not burst during baking.

Put them in a baking dish, spoon over the honey and place a piece of butter on top of each apple. Sprinkle over the spices and bake in a moderate oven (350°F) for 25–40 minutes, depending on the size and variety of the apples or until they are tender. Serve hot.

Braised Red Cabbage

1 head red cabbage, shredded
2 tablespoons butter
1 onion, sliced
2 tart apples, pared, cored and sliced
2–3 tablespoons wine vinegar
1$\frac{1}{2}$ tablespoons sugar
salt and pepper
2–3 tablespoons water
kneaded butter (made with 2 tablespoons butter and 1 tablespoon flour)

Braised cabbage is even better cooked the day before and reheated well before serving.

Method
Blanch the cabbage in a kettle of boiling water for 1 minute; drain. (The cabbage will turn deep violet at this point but when the vinegar is added it will return to its original color.)

In a flameproof casserole melt the butter and fry the onion until it is soft but not browned. Add the apples, cook 2–3 minutes longer and remove from the pot.

Add cabbage in layers with the apple mixture, sprinkling the layers with vinegar, sugar, salt, pepper and water. Cover with buttered brown paper and the lid and braise in a moderately low oven (325°F) for 1$\frac{1}{2}$–2 hours or until the cabbage is very tender. Stir the cabbage occasionally and moisten with a little extra water if necessary.

Stir in the kneaded butter a little at a time, adding just enough to thicken the cabbage juices slightly. Adjust seasoning.

Note: all recipes on pages 44–53 serve 6–8 people.

Onions in Cream

24 small onions
2 tablespoons butter
2 tablespoons flour
1 cup light cream
½ teaspoon salt
dash of ground cloves
1 tablespoon chopped parsley

Method

Peel the onions and cut a cross in the bases (this helps keep the onions whole). Cover with cold salted water and bring to a boil. Reduce heat and simmer about 10–15 minutes, depending on size, until the onions are tender when tested with a fork; drain.

In a saucepan melt the butter and stir in the flour off the heat. Stir in the cream and bring to a boil, stirring constantly, until the sauce thickens. Simmer 2 minutes. Remove from the heat and stir in the salt, cloves and parsley. Pour over the onions before serving.

Glazed Onions and Chestnuts

16–18 small onions, peeled
1 lb fresh chestnuts, skinned
   (see page 49)
1–1½ cups stock
¼ cup butter
2 tablespoons sugar
salt and pepper

Method

Put the chestnuts in a pan with 1 cup stock, cover and simmer 30–40 minutes or until the chestnuts are tender and the stock is absorbed — add more stock if the pan becomes dry.

Blanch the onions by putting in cold water, bringing to a boil and draining them.

In a skillet melt the butter, add the onions, sprinkle over the sugar with a little salt and pepper and cook over low heat, shaking occasionally, for 10 minutes or until the onions are tender and brown with caramelized sugar.

Add the chestnuts, stir carefully with the onions and cook 1–2 minutes until the chestnuts also are glazed.

Braised Celery

bunch of celery
1 large onion, diced
1 large carrot, diced
2 tablespoons butter
1 cup well-flavored stock
salt and pepper
bouquet garni

Method

Wash the celery and slice off some of the leaves. Split the bunch in four and blanch in boiling salted water; drain and cut in 3 inch lengths.

In a large flameproof casserole sweat the onion and carrot in the butter by covering tightly with foil and the lid and cooking over very low heat for 5–7 minutes or until the vegetables are soft but not browned.

Put the celery, stock, salt, pepper and the bouquet garni in with the vegetables. Cover and braise in a moderately low oven (325°F), basting from time to time, for 1–1½ hours or until the celery is tender. When cooked, the sauce should be well reduced and the celery glazed.

Strain the sauce and pour over the celery in a vegetable dish.

Baked Acorn Squash

2 large acorn squash
4 slices of bacon
salt and pepper
2–3 teaspoons brown sugar

Method

Set oven at moderate (350°F).

Wash the squash and cut them in half. Scoop out the seeds and fibers from the cavity.

Put the bacon in a shallow baking dish and bake in heated oven until crisp. Remove from the dish and drain on paper towels.

Season the squash with salt and pepper and place the halves, cut side down, in the bacon fat. Bake in heated oven for about 1 hour or until the squash are tender when tested with a fork.

Turn over, sprinkle them lightly with brown sugar, brush with some of the bacon fat, and put the crumbled bacon into the squash cavities.

Buttered Turnips

1 large yellow turnip, peeled
1 medium potato, peeled
2–3 tablespoons butter
salt and pepper
1½–2 cups hot half and half

Method

Cut the turnip and potato into even-sized pieces and cook in boiling salted water for 15–20 minutes or until tender when tested with the point of a fine knife or trussing needle. Drain, return to the pan and cook a few minutes over low heat until dry. Take from heat, add the butter with seasoning to taste and mash with a potato masher or fork until smooth. Beat in half and half.

If prepared ahead, beat in 1 cup half and half and pour over the remainder. Do not stir but replace the lid and keep the pan in a warm place for up to 30 minutes. The turnips will absorb liquid on standing.

Just before serving, beat the turnips over the heat with a wooden spoon until soft and smooth, adding more hot half and half if necessary.

Scalloped Oysters

1 quart shucked oysters, with
   their liquor
¼ cup light cream
1 cup fresh white breadcrumbs
2 cups cracker crumbs
1 cup butter, melted
salt and pepper
2 teaspoons paprika

Baking dish (2 quart capacity)

Method

Set oven at hot (425°F).

Drain the oysters, combine their liquor with the cream and set aside.

Mix the bread and cracker crumbs with the melted butter and sprinkle a thin layer on the bottom of the baking dish. Cover with half the oysters and half of the liquor and cream mixture and sprinkle lightly with salt and pepper.

Cover with a second layer of crumbs, the remaining oysters and liquor and cream. Add more salt and pepper. Finish with the remaining crumbs and sprinkle with paprika.

Watchpoint: do not make more than two layers of oysters because the middle layer will not cook.

Bake in heated oven for 25–30 minutes or until browned.

PARTY PIES

Few desserts can rival a really good homemade pie and these are some of the best.

You will find features on how to make pie and rich pie pastry in Volume 1, and flaky pastry in Volume 2.

Rum Pie

2 cup quantity of rich pie pastry (made with 2 cups flour, $\frac{1}{2}$ teaspoon salt, $\frac{2}{3}$ cup butter, 2 teaspoons sugar, 1 egg yolk and 3–4 tablespoons cold water)

For filling
$\frac{1}{3}$ cup rum
$1\frac{1}{2}$ cups milk
$\frac{1}{2}$ teaspoon ground nutmeg
3 eggs, separated
$\frac{1}{2}$ cup sugar
pinch of salt
1 envelope gelatin
$\frac{1}{4}$ cup cold water

For topping
2 teaspoons rum
$1\frac{1}{2}$ squares ($1\frac{1}{2}$ oz) semisweet chocolate
$1\frac{1}{2}$ tablespoons water
1 cup heavy cream, stiffly whipped
1 tablespoon sugar

9 inch flan ring or pie pan with removable base

Method
Make the pastry dough and chill 30 minutes. Set oven at hot (400°F).

Roll out the dough, line the flan ring or pie pan and bake blind in heated oven for 10 minutes. Turn down heat to moderately hot (375°F), bake 12–15 minutes longer or until brown. Cool the pastry shell.

To prepare the filling: scald the milk with the nutmeg.

Beat the egg yolks, sugar and salt until thick and light, stir in the milk, return the mixture to the pan and cook over low heat, stirring constantly, until the custard thickens slightly and coats the back of a spoon. Do not let it boil.

Sprinkle the gelatin over the cold water in a small pan and let stand 5 minutes or until spongy. Stir into the hot custard and leave to cool; stir occasionally. Chill the mixture in the refrigerator or over a pan of ice water.

Beat the egg whites until they hold a stiff peak, and when the custard mixture starts to thicken add the rum, then fold in the egg whites. Pour into the pastry shell and chill until set.

To prepare the topping: melt the chocolate in the water over low heat, stirring, then cool. Divide the whipped cream in half; flavor one half with sugar and the other with rum. Mix the cold but still liquid chocolate with the rum-flavored cream.

Cover the pie with the sugar-flavored cream, then spread the chocolate cream on top. Chill and serve within 1–2 hours.

Top rum pie with sweetened whipped cream, then with rum-flavored chocolate cream; chill before serving

Pecan Pie

1 cup quantity of pie pastry (made with 1 cup flour, pinch of salt, $\frac{1}{3}$ cup shortening and 2–3 tablespoons cold water)

For filling
$1\frac{1}{2}$ cups coarsely broken pecans
$\frac{1}{4}$ cup butter
1 cup dark brown sugar
3 eggs
$\frac{1}{2}$ cup dark corn syrup
1 teaspoon vanilla
pinch of salt

9 inch pie pan

Method
Make the pastry dough and chill 30 minutes. Roll it out and line pie pan; flute the edge and chill again.

Set oven at moderately hot (375°F).

To prepare the filling: cream the butter, add the sugar and beat until soft and light. Beat in the eggs, one at a time, then stir in the corn syrup, pecans, vanilla and salt.

Pour the filling into the pie shell and bake in heated oven for 40 minutes or until a knife inserted in the center comes out clean. Serve hot or cold.

To cook pumpkin: cut the pumpkin in half cross-wise and scoop out the seeds and fibers. Place the halves in a roasting pan, shell side up. Bake in a moderately low oven (325°F) for 1 hour or more, depending on size, or until very tender.

Scoop out the flesh, work through a sieve or food mill or purée in a blender.

Note: all recipes on pages 44–53 serve 6–8 people.

Pumpkin Pie (1)

1 cup quantity of pie pastry
(made with 1 cup flour, pinch
of salt, $\frac{1}{3}$ cup shortening and
2–3 tablespoons cold water)

For filling
1$\frac{1}{2}$ cups cooked, puréed
pumpkin (see box)
$\frac{3}{4}$ cup dark brown sugar
2 tablespoons honey
grated rind and juice of 1 lemon
grated rind and juice of
1 orange
3 eggs, beaten to mix

For topping
1 cup heavy cream, stiffly
whipped
2 teaspoons sugar
$\frac{1}{4}$ teaspoon grated nutmeg
$\frac{3}{4}$ cup coarsely chopped
walnuts or pecans

9 inch pie pan

Method
Make the pastry dough and
chill 30 minutes. Roll it out
and line the pie pan, pressing
up the edge of the dough with
the thumb or finger, then
fluting with 2 fingers and a
thumb to form a high edge.
Chill.

Set oven at moderately hot
(375°F).

To prepare the filling: mix
the sugar, honey, fruit juices
and rinds and stir in the eggs.
Stir the mixture into the
pumpkin purée and pour into
the pie shell.

Bake the pie in the heated
oven for 45–55 minutes or
until a knife inserted in the
center comes out clean. Cool
thoroughly.

An hour or two before
serving prepare the topping.
Stir the sugar and nutmeg
into the whipped cream and
spread it on the pie. Sprinkle
with chopped nuts and chill.

Pumpkin pie (1) is topped with chopped nuts

Pumpkin Pie (2)

1 cup quantity of pie pastry
(made with 1 cup flour, pinch
of salt, $\frac{1}{3}$ cup shortening and
2–3 tablespoons cold water)

For filling
1$\frac{1}{2}$ cups cooked, puréed
pumpkin (see box)
$\frac{3}{4}$ cup dark brown sugar
pinch of salt
1$\frac{1}{2}$ teaspoons ground cinnamon
$\frac{1}{2}$ teaspoon ground ginger
$\frac{1}{4}$ teaspoon ground cloves
3 eggs, beaten to mix
2 cups light cream

9 inch pie pan

Method
Make the pastry dough and
chill 30 minutes. Roll it out
and line the pie pan, pressing
up the edge of the dough with
the thumb or finger, then
fluting with 2 fingers and a
thumb to form a high edge.
Chill.

Set oven at moderately hot
(375°F).

To prepare the filling: mix
the sugar, salt and spices
together. Stir the beaten eggs
into the puréed pumpkin, then
add the sugar and spice mixture and the cream. Mix until
smooth and pour into the pie
shell.

Bake the pie in heated
oven for 45–50 minutes or
until a knife inserted in the
filling comes out clean. Serve
warm or cold.

Apple Florentine

1$\frac{1}{2}$ cup quantity of flaky pastry
(made with 1$\frac{1}{2}$ cups flour,
pinch of salt, $\frac{1}{4}$ cup butter,
$\frac{1}{4}$ cup shortening and 6–8
tablespoons ice water)
confectioners' sugar (for
sprinkling)

For spiced ale or cider
1 cup ale or cider
$\frac{1}{4}$ teaspoon grated nutmeg
1 inch piece of cinnamon stick
$\frac{1}{4}$ teaspoon ground ginger
3–4 strips of lemon rind
6 tablespoons dark brown
sugar

For filling
5–6 Golden Delicious or other
crisp dessert apples, pared,
cored and quartered
$\frac{1}{4}$ cup butter
$\frac{1}{2}$ cup granulated sugar
1 teaspoon ground cinnamon
grated rind of 1 lemon

*Deep 9–10 inch pie pan or
baking dish*

A 'Florentine', the forerunner
of today's fruit pie, was a
covered pie without a bottom
crust made in a deeper pan
than is now customary.

Method
Make the pastry dough and
chill 30 minutes.

Set oven at hot (400°F).

To spice the ale or cider:
pour it into a saucepan and
add the other ingredients.
Heat slowly until the sugar
has dissolved; strain and cool.

To prepare the filling: melt
the butter in a skillet, add the
apples, sprinkle them with
4–6 tablespoons of the sugar
and turn them over. Fry over
medium heat until the apples
are just tender and the sugar
has caramelized to a golden
brown. Add the cinnamon
and lemon rind and arrange
the filling in the pan or dish.
Moisten with some of the
spiced ale or cider and cool.

Roll out the dough to about
three-eighths inch thickness,
lay over the filling, trim the
edge and scallop it. Sprinkle
with the remaining sugar and
bake in heated oven for 25–30
minutes or until the pastry is
crisp and brown.

Run a sharp knife around
the edge to lift off the crust;
cut it into serving portions.
Moisten the apples with more
ale or cider unless they are
already very moist, replace
the pieces of crust and
sprinkle generously with
confectioners' sugar. Serve
hot or cold.

Make a sparkling Rhine wine cup to please your holiday guests

PARTY DRINKS

Here are some drinks, mild or potent, which will help to make the party go. Be sure the hot ones are very hot and the cold ones very cold. Do not use an aluminum pan for heating punches because it may give the mixture a metallic flavor. If you are pouring hot punch into a glass punch bowl, be sure the bowl is warm and set it on a wooden board to avoid cracking.

COLD DRINKS

Rum Punch

2 cups rum
1 cup brandy
$\frac{1}{4}$ cup orange-flavored liqueur (Curaçao, Triple Sec, Grand Marnier)
$\frac{1}{2}$ cup orange juice
$\frac{1}{2}$ cup lemon juice
2 cups freshly made tea, chilled
$\frac{1}{4}$ cup superfine (bar) sugar
orange slices (for garnish)

Serves 8–10 people.

Method
Over a large piece of ice in a punch bowl pour the rum, brandy, orange-flavored liqueur and fruit juices. Mix thoroughly, leave 15 minutes or until well chilled and remove the ice. Stir in the tea and sugar. Serve in punch glasses, garnished with a slice of orange.

Stirrup Cup

2 cups rum
1 cup fresh pineapple juice
juice of 2 limes
1 tablespoon brown sugar
few ice cubes
rind of 2 lemons, peeled in one piece

Serves 6 people.

Method
Half fill a pitcher with cracked ice and pour over the rum, pineapple juice, lime juice and sugar. Stir well until the sugar has dissolved and strain into a smaller pitcher or punch bowl. Add a few ice cubes and the lemon rind and serve.

Rhine Wine Cup

2 bottles of white Rhine wine (Germany or California)
3 tablespoons orange-flavored liqueur (Curaçao, Triple Sec, Grand Marnier)
$\frac{1}{4}$ cup brandy
good dash of bitters
about $1\frac{1}{2}$ cups club soda
few slices of fresh fruit (apple, orange, strawberries, pineapple, etc.)
2–3 sprigs of fresh mint, bruised
sugar (to taste) – optional
few ice cubes

Serves 10–12 people.

Method
Mix all the ingredients together (except the soda and ice) about 1 hour before serving. Add the soda and ice before serving.

Claret Cup

2 bottles of red Bordeaux wine (claret)
$\frac{1}{4}$ cup brandy
3 tablespoons orange-flavored liqueur (Curaçao, Triple Sec, Grand Marnier)
1 orange, sliced
$1\frac{1}{2}$ tablespoons sugar
2–3 sprigs of fresh mint, bruised
10–12 slices of cucumber
1 teaspoon bitters
1 pint club soda
few ice cubes

Serves 10–12 people.

Method
Mix all the ingredients together except the soda and ice cubes in a large pitcher or punch bowl. Chill well and add the soda and ice cubes just before serving.

Champagne Cup

1 bottle of Champagne
3 tablespoons orange-flavored liqueur (Curaçao, Triple Sec, Grand Marnier)
$\frac{1}{2}$ cup brandy
2–3 teaspoons superfine (bar) sugar
1 pint club soda, chilled
good dash of bitters
few slices of fresh fruit (apple, orange, strawberries, pineapple)
2–3 sprigs of fresh mint, bruised
few ice cubes

Serves 6–8 people.

Method
Chill the Champagne thoroughly before opening. Mix it in a punch bowl with the orange-flavored liqueur and brandy and stir in sugar to taste. Add the soda, bitters, fresh fruit, mint and ice cubes and serve at once.

Hard Cider Punch

2 quarts hard cider
6 tablespoons brandy
2 oranges, each stuck with 6 cloves
2 dessert apples, sliced
1–2 tablespoons sugar (or to taste)

Serves 10–12 people.

Method
Pour the cider into a large saucepan and add the other ingredients. Simmer 20–30 minutes and let cool. Pour the punch into a punch bowl and serve.

Whiskey Milk Punch

1 cup whiskey
6 cups milk
$\frac{1}{4}$ cup superfine (bar) sugar
ground nutmeg (for sprinkling)

Serves 6–8 people.

Method
In a punch bowl, pour the milk over a large piece of ice, add sugar, stir until dissolved and leave 15 minutes or until chilled. Add the whiskey, stir well, remove the ice, sprinkle with nutmeg and serve.

Rum or Brandy Milk Punch

Make as for whiskey milk punch, substituting 1 cup of rum or brandy for the whiskey.

Simple milk punch is made with whiskey, sugar and milk

Simple Milk Punch

6 cups milk
1½ cups whiskey
2 tablespoons superfine (bar) sugar
little grated nutmeg (for sprinkling)
ice cubes

Serves 6 people.

Method
Mix the milk, whiskey and sugar in a punch bowl, stir until the sugar is dissolved and chill.

Just before serving, add ice cubes. Serve the punch in mugs or glasses and sprinkle each one with a little grated nutmeg.

Spiced Milk Punch

4 cups milk, chilled
1 cup rum
2 tablespoons superfine (bar) sugar
1 teaspoon ground cinnamon
1 teaspoon ground allspice
½ teaspoon ground cloves
½ teaspoon ground nutmeg
ice cubes

Serves 4—6 people.

Method
In a punch bowl mix the rum, sugar and spices, cover and let stand 4—5 hours.

Just before serving, pour in the milk and add the ice cubes.

HOT DRINKS

Claret Punch

2 bottles of red Bordeaux wine
 (claret)
1 orange
1 lemon, thickly sliced and
 stuck with 6 cloves
3 inch piece of cinnamon stick
12 sugar cubes
½ cup brandy

Serves 10–12 people.

Method
Bake the orange in a moderately hot oven (375°F) for 30 minutes or until well browned.

Pour the claret into a saucepan, add the lemon, cinnamon stick, baked orange and half the sugar. Bring almost to a boil and infuse over very low heat, just below simmering point, for 15 minutes uncovered.

Pour the liquid into a warmed punch bowl and remove the cinnamon stick.

Put the brandy in a small saucepan with the remaining sugar, heat slowly until the sugar has dissolved, then flame the brandy. Leave a few seconds, pour into the punch bowl and serve.

Cardinal's Punch

1 bottle of Champagne
2 large oranges, each stuck
 with 8 cloves
¼ cup sugar

Serves 6 people.

Method
Bake the oranges in a moderately hot oven (375°F) for 30 minutes or until well browned. Cut them in quarters

and remove the seeds.

Combine the oranges in a saucepan with the Champagne and sugar and heat the mixture slowly until a froth appears on the top — it should be very hot but not boiling. Pour into a warmed punch bowl and serve with a piece of the orange in each glass.

Whiskey Punch

1 quart whiskey
thinly peeled rind and strained
 juice of 2 large lemons
½ lb sugar cubes
2 quarts boiling water

Serves 15 people.

Method
Put the lemon rind and juice with the sugar in a punch bowl. Pour on the boiling water and stir until the sugar has dissolved. Stand the whiskey in a pan of hot but not boiling water to warm through, then add it to the hot liquid. Stir well and serve.

Bishop

1 bottle of port
1 orange, stuck with 6 cloves
2–3 tablespoons sugar
 (optional)

This quantity of bishop may be diluted with 1–1½ cups water. Serves 6–8 people.

Method
Cut the orange in half and put in a saucepan with the port and a little sugar, if you like. Heat gently and, when at simmering point, flame, letting the mixture burn for several seconds. Then pour it into a warmed punch bowl.

The name **bishop** comes from Northern Europe, where any hot spiced wine is called 'Bischof'. In England, undergraduates refer to hot mulled port as 'bishop'.

On this side of the Atlantic, cranberries, strawberries, blueberries or raspberries are often added and the bishop becomes more like a dessert that can be served hot or cold.

Cranberry Bishop

4 cups (1 lb) cranberries
1 bottle of sweet white wine
1 inch piece of cinnamon stick
½ cup sugar
juice of 1 lime
½ cup brandy

Serves 6 people.

Method
Wash and pick over the cranberries. Put 1 cup of them with 1 cup of white wine, the cinnamon stick and ¼ cup sugar in a saucepan and simmer 5–6 minutes or until the cranberries are very soft. Remove the cinnamon stick and work cranberries and liquid through a fine sieve or purée them in a blender.

Add the remaining sugar and lime juice and simmer 2–3 minutes.

Cook the remaining cranberries in 1 cup of white wine for 4–5 minutes or until the berries are just tender. Stir into the cranberry purée.

Just before serving, add the remaining white wine with the brandy and serve in stemmed glasses with a spoon.

If you want to serve cold cranberry bishop, proceed as follows: after simmering sugar and lime juice, chill

thoroughly. Cook remaining cranberries as in the recipe but cool before stirring into cranberry purée. Chill at least 2 hours. Finish as in the recipe and serve with lady fingers.

Café Brûlot

4 cups hot demitasse coffee
⅓ cup brandy
6 sugar cubes
1 tangerine
3 inch piece of cinnamon stick
4–5 cloves

Serves 6 people.

Method
Rub the sugar cubes over the tangerine rind to absorb the zest (oil). Put the sugar, brandy, cinnamon and cloves in a saucepan, heat slowly, then flame the brandy and let it burn out.

Pour on the very hot coffee, stir well and strain into warm demitasse cups.

Irish Coffee

½ cup Irish whiskey
4 cups hot demitasse coffee
sugar (to taste)
½ cup heavy cream

Serves 6 people.

Method
Warm stemmed glasses and pour a little whiskey into each. Fill up with very hot coffee and add sugar to taste. Pour a tablespoon of cream (over the back of a spoon) onto the surface of the coffee. Serve at once without stirring.

Use leftovers of turkey, capon or chicken to make salad parisienne

IDEAS FOR POULTRY LEFTOVERS

Poultry leftovers can look and taste as good as the original dish, but don't bring a half-finished turkey carcass to your table. Instead carve the meat in slices and arrange these on a platter with a garnish. To pep up the flavor, add pickles and relishes, or enrich the meat by mixing it with mayonnaise and chopped peppers and onion. Or serve the meat hot in a curry or deviled sauce.

Since leftover meat is already cooked, reheat it at high heat for a short time only. The meat may be left in a sauce for a few minutes to absorb flavors, but always heat it thoroughly first.

Keep the carcass of a bird to make excellent stock for sauces, soups and for casseroles.

All the following turkey recipes are equally good for capon or chicken.

Salad Parisienne

2 cups cooked turkey, cut in strips
4 red dessert apples, wiped, cored and thinly sliced
6 oz (1½ cups) sliced Gruyère cheese, cut in strips
1 head of Boston or romaine lettuce
1 tablespoon chopped parsley

For dressing
6 tablespoons oil
¼ cup heavy cream
2 tablespoons white wine vinegar
salt and pepper

Method
Combine the ingredients for the dressing, whisk until slightly thickened and season to taste.

Mix the turkey, apples and cheese together. Wash the lettuce and arrange the leaves around a salad bowl. Pile the turkey mixture in the center, spoon over the dressing, cover and chill ½–1 hour. Just before serving, sprinkle with chopped parsley.

Turkey Croquettes

2 cups cooked turkey, diced or chopped
1 envelope gelatin
¼ cup water
thick béchamel sauce, made with 3 tablespoons butter, 3 tablespoons flour and 1½ cups milk (infused with slice of onion, 6 peppercorns, blade of mace, bay leaf)
1 egg yolk
salt and pepper
deep fat (for frying)

For coating
1 egg, beaten to mix with ½ teaspoon olive oil
1 cup dry white breadcrumbs

For serving
hollandaise sauce or tomato sauce
fried parsley (for garnish)

Deep fat thermometer (optional)

Method
In a small pan sprinkle the gelatin over the water and leave 5 minutes until spongy. Stir into the béchamel sauce while it is still hot. Add the turkey meat with the egg yolk and season the mixture well. Spread it about 1–1½ inches thick in ice cube trays, cover and chill until very firm.

Cut the mixture in even pieces and roll or pat on a floured board into cylinders or patties, using two metal spatulas. When the surface is smooth without cracks, brush with beaten egg and roll in breadcrumbs.

Heat the deep fat and dip the frying basket into it to prevent the croquettes from sticking. Lift the basket out, place several croquettes in the basket and when the fat reaches 360°F–370°F on a fat thermometer, lower the basket gently into it. Fry croquettes until golden brown, then drain on paper towels. Keep warm while frying the remaining croquettes.

Watchpoint: do not fry the croquettes for too long or they will burst.

Serve with hollandaise or tomato sauce and garnish with fried parsley.

Turkey Curry

3 cups cooked turkey, diced or cut in strips
¼ cup butter
2 onions, finely chopped
2 stalks of celery, chopped
1 tart apple, pared, cored and diced
1 clove of garlic, crushed
1 tablespoon curry powder
½ teaspoon ground allspice
½ teaspoon ground ginger
¼ teaspoon ground coriander
1 tablespoon flour
1 cup chicken or turkey stock
1 cup white wine
2 tablespoons chopped parsley

Method
Melt the butter and cook the onions and celery over low heat until soft. Add the apple, garlic, curry powder, spices and flour and continue to cook, stirring, for 2 minutes.

Stir in the stock and white wine, bring to a boil and simmer 10–15 minutes or until the sauce is fairly thick. Add the turkey, bring to a boil, cover pan and let stand 15 minutes in a warm place for the flavors to blend.

Spoon the curry into a serving dish, sprinkle with chopped parsley and serve with boiled rice.

Deviled Goose or Turkey

6–8 large pieces of cooked goose or dark turkey meat
½–¾ cup melted butter
1 teaspoon prepared mustard
1 teaspoon Dijon-style mustard
1 teaspoon Worcestershire sauce
¼ teaspoon cayenne
¼ teaspoon salt
6 tablespoons browned breadcrumbs

Method
Score the meat deeply with a pointed knife and dip the pieces in melted butter. Mix together the prepared and Dijon-style mustards, Worcestershire sauce, cayenne and salt and rub over the meat, pressing well into the cuts. Leave ½–1 hour.

Heat the broiler, lay the meat on a baking sheet, scatter over the breadcrumbs and sprinkle with remaining melted butter. Broil 7–8 minutes or until browned, turning once and basting the meat often with butter.

Turkey Divan

2–3 cups cooked turkey, cut in strips
1 bunch of fresh broccoli or 2 packages frozen broccoli

For mornay sauce
3 tablespoons butter
3 tablespoons flour
2 cups milk
½ cup grated Parmesan cheese
pinch of nutmeg
salt and pepper

Method
Peel the thick stems of fresh broccoli with a vegetable peeler to remove the hard outside skin, trim the ends and cut large stems in half.

Cook broccoli in boiling salted water for 8–10 minutes or until tender. Drain, refresh and drain again. Cook frozen broccoli according to package directions.

To make sauce: in a saucepan melt butter, stir in flour off the heat and pour in the milk. Bring to a boil, stirring, and cook 2 minutes. Take from the heat and stir in half the cheese with nutmeg and seasoning to taste.

Arrange the broccoli and turkey in layers in a buttered baking dish and spoon the mornay sauce over the top. Sprinkle over the remaining grated cheese and bake in a moderately hot oven (375°F) for 15 minutes or until very hot and browned.

Turkey Mousse

2 cups ground turkey meat
1 envelope gelatin
1½ cups chicken or turkey stock
3 egg yolks
¼ teaspoon nutmeg
2 tablespoons sherry
salt and pepper
½ cup mayonnaise
1 cup heavy cream, whipped
    until it holds a soft shape
bunch of watercress
    (for garnish)

Ring mold (1½ quart capacity)

Method
Lightly oil the mold.

In a small pan sprinkle the gelatin over ½ cup stock and let stand 5 minutes or until spongy. Stir the remaining stock into the egg yolks and cook over low heat until the mixture thickens slightly. Take from heat and stir in the softened gelatin until dissolved.

Stir in the turkey meat with nutmeg, sherry and seasoning to taste. Chill over a pan of ice

water, stirring occasionally, until the mixture starts to set. Stir in the mayonnaise, then fold in the whipped cream and pour the mixture into the mold. Chill 2 hours or until firm.

Just before serving, turn out onto a platter and garnish with watercress.

To turn out the mousse: lower it into a pan of hand-hot water so the water just reaches the top edge. Leave it a few seconds, easing the mousse gently sideways with your fingers to make sure it is loose. Lift out the mold and wipe off any water with a cloth. Hold the platter over the mold, then quickly turn both over together.

Set the platter on the table and, holding both mold and platter firmly, give a sharp shake sideways. The mousse will drop onto the platter. Lift off the mold carefully and wipe around the edge of the platter before serving.

Turkey and Mushroom Loaf

2 lb loaf crusty white bread
3 tablespoons melted butter
1 egg, beaten to mix

For filling
2 cups cooked turkey, cut in
    strips
2 cups (½ lb) mushrooms, sliced
3–4 tablespoons butter
1 onion, finely chopped
1½ tablespoons flour
1 cup chicken stock
salt and pepper
1 teaspoon mixed herbs (thyme,
    tarragon)
pinch of ground nutmeg
1 tablespoon chopped parsley

Method
Set oven at moderate (350°F).

Cut the top off the loaf

Turkey and mushroom loaf is an ideal way of using up leftover poultry

and scoop out the soft inside with a spoon. Brush inside of the loaf and lid with melted butter, then with beaten egg. Bake in heated oven for 7–10 minutes or until the bread is crisp and brown.

To make the filling: melt 2 tablespoons butter and fry the onion until soft but not browned. Stir in the flour and cook until it is straw-colored. Take from the heat and pour in the stock. Season, bring to a boil, stirring, and simmer 2–3 minutes. Take from heat and add the mixed herbs, nutmeg, parsley and turkey pieces. Sauté the mushrooms in the remaining butter until they are tender.

Spread a layer of mushrooms in the bottom of the loaf, add the turkey mixture and arrange the remaining mushrooms on top. Replace the lid and bake in heated oven for 8–10 minutes longer or until the loaf is very hot.

Spread a layer of mushrooms in bottom of the baked loaf, add turkey mixture and arrange remaining mushrooms on top

Set this elegant buffet table (from left to right): ham and mushroom bouchées, galantine of turkey and cold roast beef; shrimp and egg mousse, corn and pickled onion salad, beet and horseradish relish, celery and green bean salad; gâteau Diane, decorated with chocolate caraque, and fruit compote

ENTERTAIN WITH AN ELEGANT BUFFET

Entertaining large numbers is easy if you follow the advice for this week's buffet. We suggest a colorful and varied menu with dishes chosen to appeal to every taste. Whether you make all of the dishes or just a few, you'll find quantities and instructions easy to follow and, with the help of the Timetable, you can create a sumptuous buffet for 30–60 people.

With so diverse a group of foods, it is best to offer both red and white wines. A semi-dry Vouvray from the Loire, or its California counterpart, Chenin Blanc, will complement the shrimp and turkey dishes nicely. Those guests who favor sweetbreads or beef will appreciate a Beaujolais-type wine — whether it is from Burgundy or California. As is so often the case, a rosé wine will not do as a compromise — it has neither the delicacy to escort the mousse nor the authority to stand beside the beef.

Shrimp & Egg Mousse
Ham & Mushroom Bouchées
Galantine of Turkey   Cold Roast Beef

Belgian Endive & Orange Salad
Celery & Green Bean Salad
Corn & Pickled Onion Salad
Potato Salad
Beet & Horseradish Relish

Gâteau Mille Feuilles au Citron
Gâteau Diane   Fruit Compote

∽

White wine — Vouvray (Loire)
or Chenin Blanc (California)
Red wine — Beaujolais (Burgundy or California)

TIMETABLE

Several days before

Make puff pastry dough and chill. Bake bouchées, and bases, rings and decoration for gâteaux mille feuilles and, when cool, store in an airtight container.

Make meringue rounds and store, layered with wax paper, in an airtight container.

Make aspic and stock for galantine.

Make the mayonnaise and vinaigrette dressing and store in airtight containers in the refrigerator.

Day before

Make shrimp and egg mousse and leave covered in the mold.

Make galantine and refrigerate.

Make filling for bouchées, cover and chill.

Slice galantine, cover with aspic and chill. When set, cover with plastic wrap.

Make filling and complete gâteau Diane but do not decorate with caraque. Cover and keep in refrigerator. Make chocolate caraque and store in an airtight container.

Make lemon curd and apricot jam glaze for gâteaux mille feuilles.

Morning

Prepare the filling and decoration for the mousse, cover and refrigerate.

Roast beef and cool it but do not refrigerate unless the kitchen is very hot.

For endive and orange salad: slice or quarter endive, section or slice oranges and refrigerate.

For celery and green bean salad: cut celery and soak in ice water. Cook, drain and chill beans.

Make beet and horseradish relish and cover.

For corn and pickled onion salad: combine corn and onion with seasonings, pile in a bowl and refrigerate.

For potato salad: cook potatoes, add vinaigrette dressing. Cover and chill.

Put puff pastry rings together for gâteaux mille feuilles but do not make filling.

Set the table.

Afternoon

Complete the corn and pickled onion and potato salads.

Complete the filling, fill and decorate mille feuilles.

Decorate gâteaux Diane with caraque.

Make the fruit compote.

Unmold the mousse, fill the center, decorate and cover with plastic wrap.

Half an hour before serving

Heat bouchées in oven and the filling in a water bath.

Complete the celery and green bean, and endive and orange salads.

Set the food on the table.

Fill the bouchées and serve.

QUANTITIES FOR 60 GUESTS

The dishes in this menu, when combined, will serve 60 people. If you prefer, choose just a few of them and make those in larger quantities. Many dishes can be doubled or tripled but for some recipes it is safer to make several batches of a single quantity, as suggested below.

Shrimp and egg mousse: each mousse serves about 10, so make 3 for 30 people.

Ham and mushroom bouchées: recipe makes about 30 cases with filling.

Galantine of turkey: a 12 lb turkey makes about 25–30 servings.

Cold roast beef: a whole rib roast weighing about 20 lb serves 30 people.

Gâteau Diane: each gâteau serves 10, so make 3 separate ones for 30 people.

Gâteau mille feuilles au citron: recipe makes 3 gâteaux, each one serving 10.

Fruit compote: makes 10–15 servings.

Salads: each of the four salad recipes, right, make 20–25 servings.

You will find that **cooking times** given in the individual recipes for these dishes have sometimes been adapted in the timetable to help you when cooking and serving this menu as a party meal.

Belgian Endive and Orange Salad

Trim the bases and outer leaves from 3 lb Belgian endive and split the stalks in quarters or cut in ¾ inch diagonal slices. Toss endive with 6 oranges, peeled and sectioned or sliced, and 1 cup vinaigrette dressing.

Celery and Green Bean Salad

Combine 4 lb cooked and sliced green beans with 6 celery hearts, cut in julienne strips and soaked in ice water until crisp. Toss with 1½ cups vinaigrette dressing.

Corn and Pickled Onion Salad

Drain 2 cans (16 oz each) of whole kernel corn, 3 jars (8½ oz each) pickled onions and 1 small can pimiento, chopped. Combine and toss with 1 cup vinaigrette dressing.

Potato Salad

Cook 7 lb potatoes in their skins until tender. Drain and, when cool enough to handle, peel and cut into cubes. While potatoes are still warm, spoon over 2 cups vinaigrette dressing. When cold, mix with 2 cups mayonnaise and salt and pepper to taste. Arrange in a serving dish; coat with 2 cups more mayonnaise.

Ham and Mushroom Bouchées

4 cup quantity of puff pastry
  (see page 74)
egg glaze (see page 74)

For filling
1 lb lean cooked ham, diced
2 cups ($\frac{1}{2}$ lb) mushrooms, diced
1 tablespoon butter
juice of 1 lemon
$\frac{1}{2}$ cup water
2 cups béchamel sauce, made
  with $\frac{1}{4}$ cup butter, $\frac{1}{4}$ cup
  flour, and 2 cups milk
  (infused with slice of onion,
  blade of mace,
  6 peppercorns, $\frac{1}{2}$ bay leaf)
$\frac{1}{2}$ cup heavy cream
salt and pepper

*Cookie cutters (2$\frac{1}{2}$ and 1$\frac{1}{2}$ inch
  diameter)*

Method
Set oven at hot (425°F).

Roll out the pastry dough, glaze it, cut out bouchées with the cookie cutters, and bake them (see page 74). Cool a little, take off the lids with the point of a knife and scoop out the soft centers with a tea-spoon. When completely cool, store in an airtight container.

To make the filling: put the diced mushrooms with the butter, lemon juice and water in a pan, cover and cook over high heat for 2 minutes. Cool.

Make the béchamel sauce, stir in the liquid from the mushrooms with the cream and bring just to a boil. Add the ham and diced mushrooms and season the mixture to taste. Cover and chill until needed.

To heat, set the bouchées on a baking sheet. Reheat in a moderate oven (350°F) for 10 minutes or until very hot. Reheat the filling in the top of a double boiler or in a water bath.

To serve, fill the bouchées and replace the lids on a slant. Serve at once.

Galantine of Turkey

12 lb turkey
$\frac{1}{2}$ cup sherry
3–4 cups well-flavored stock

For stuffing
$\frac{3}{4}$ cup butter
2 onions, finely chopped
2 lb cooked ham, ground
1 lb raw veal, ground
4$\frac{1}{2}$ cups fresh white
  breadcrumbs
1 tablespoon mixed chopped
  herbs (thyme, oregano,
  marjoram)
grated rind and juice of
  2 oranges
salt and pepper
1 egg, beaten to mix

For serving
3 cups aspic, cool but still
  liquid (see pages 18–19)
bunch of watercress

Trussing needle and fine string

A galantine is made with veal, chicken or duck that is boned, spread with various stuffings, rolled up, sewn or tied secure-ly, then cooked slowly in stock and coated with aspic when cold.

Method
Bone the turkey in the same way as a chicken (see Volume 1).

To prepare the stuffing: melt the butter, stir in the chopped onions and cook until soft but not browned. Let the mixture cool. Stir in ham, veal, breadcrumbs, herbs and add the orange rind and juice. Season to taste and bind the stuffing with beaten egg.

Spread the turkey flat on a table, skin side down, and spread the stuffing over it. Roll the turkey lengthwise, sew the sides together with fine string, secure the ends to keep the stuffing in place and tie it at 2 inch intervals into a neat cylinder.

Put the galantine in a deep pan or flameproof casserole, pour over the sherry and stock and baste. Cover with the lid and simmer over low heat on top of the stove for 3–3$\frac{1}{2}$ hours or until the galantine is tender when pierced with a fork. Let cool in the liquid, then drain, wrap in foil and refrigerate.

To finish the galantine: remove all the string and cut the galantine in neat, even slices. Arrange the slices, overlapping, on a large platter and chill. Baste the slices with cool but still liquid aspic and chill until set. Cover the dish until serving, then garnish with watercress.

Beet and Horseradish Relish

6–8 large cooked beets
$\frac{1}{3}$ cup prepared horseradish
1 teaspoon dry mustard
$\frac{1}{2}$ teaspoon salt
$\frac{1}{2}$ teaspoon pepper
1 tablespoon sugar
3 tablespoons red wine vinegar
1$\frac{1}{2}$ cups sour cream

Method
Peel and grate the beets and mix them with the horse-radish. Combine the mus-tard, salt, pepper, sugar and vinegar with the sour cream and mix well. Stir into the beet mixture and transfer to a serving bowl.

Shrimp and egg mousse, the center filled with the shrimp and tomato mixture, is garnished with watercress and tomato

Shrimp and Egg Mousse

½ lb peeled, cooked shrimps
12 hard-cooked eggs
2 cups mayonnaise
1½ envelopes gelatin
¾ cup stock, white wine or water
salt and pepper
2 egg whites

For sauce
¼ cup butter
¼ cup flour
2½ cups milk (flavored with
   1 teaspoon paprika and
   1 teaspoon tomato paste)

For garnish
6 medium tomatoes, peeled,
   seeded and cut in strips
½ lb peeled, cooked shrimps
few drops of Tabasco
1 teaspoon tomato ketchup
3 tablespoons vinaigrette
   dressing (see page 27)
watercress, additional tomato
   slices, or thin cucumber
   slices

Ring mold (1½ quart capacity)

Method

Oil the mold.

Cut the hard-cooked eggs in half, remove the yolks and work them through a sieve. Chop the egg whites finely. Coarsely chop the shrimps or work through a food mill.

Make the sauce (as for béchamel) and when it is cold, mix together the shrimps, egg yolks and sauce; purée in a blender until smooth or work through a food mill and stir in the mayonnaise.

Sprinkle the gelatin over the stock, wine or water and let stand for about 5 minutes or until spongy. Dissolve it over a pan of hot water and add to the mayonnaise mixture with the finely chopped cooked egg whites. Season well with salt and pepper. Beat the uncooked egg

whites until they hold a stiff peak.

Chill the egg mixture until it begins to thicken, then fold in the beaten egg whites. Pour into the oiled mold and refrigerate at least 2 hours until set.

To prepare the garnish: combine the Tabasco and ketchup with the vinaigrette dressing and mix with the tomato strips and the whole peeled shrimps. Season highly to taste.

Not more than 1 hour before serving, turn the mousse out onto a large platter and fill the center with the tomato and shrimp mixture. Garnish the mold with watercress, additional tomato slices or thin cucumber slices.

Gâteau Diane

4 egg whites
1 cup sugar
3 squares (3 oz) semisweet
   chocolate (for caraque)

For filling
8 squares (8 oz) semisweet
   chocolate
½ cup water
2½ cups heavy cream

3 baking sheets

Method

Line the baking sheets with silicone paper. Set the oven at low (250°F–300°F).

Beat the egg whites until stiff, then gradually beat in half the sugar until the mixture is stiff and glossy. Fold in the remaining sugar. Spread the mixture into 3 thin circles about 8–9 inches in diameter on the baking sheets. Bake the meringues in heated oven for 1 hour or longer until they are dry and crisp. Cool slightly, then peel off the paper.

To make the filling: break or cut the chocolate into small pieces, put it in a pan with the water and melt it over very low heat, stirring, until smooth. Transfer the chocolate to a bowl and cool. Whip the cream until it begins to thicken, add the cooled chocolate and continue beating until thick.

To finish: spread each layer of meringue with the chocolate cream and pile one on top of the other. Spread the top and sides with the chocolate cream and decorate with the chocolate caraque.

The cake must be filled at least 2–3 hours before serving (it can even be done the day before if it is kept in the refrigerator); this keeps the meringue soft enough to be cut, but the covering of cream

prevents the meringue from becoming too soft.

For chocolate caraque: grate 3 squares (3 oz) semisweet chocolate; melt it on a plate over a pan of hot water and work with a spatula until smooth. Spread thinly on a marble or Formica-type surface; let stand until nearly set

With a long spatula or pliable sharp knife, shave the chocolate off the slab slantwise, using a gentle sawing movement and holding knife blade almost at a right angle

Decorate the gâteau Diane with the long chocolate scrolls

Gâteau mille feuilles au citron is decorated with rosettes of cream and chopped candied fruit and pistachios

Gâteau Mille Feuilles au Citron

8 cup quantity of puff pastry
   (see page 74)
apricot jam glaze, made with
   18 oz (1½ jars) apricot jam,
   juice of 1 lemon and ¼ cup
   water
6 cups heavy cream

For lemon curd filling
1 cup sugar
½ cup unsalted butter
grated rind and strained juice of
   3 lemons (to give ½ cup juice
   and 3 tablespoons rind)
3 eggs, beaten to mix

For decoration
puff pastry trimmings
candied fruit or almonds or
   pistachios

*2 pan lids (5–6 and 8–9 inches
   diameter); 2–3 baking
   sheets; pastry bag and star
   tube*

Makes 3 gâteaux.

Method
Set oven at hot (425°F) and dampen the baking sheets.

To make 3 bases and 12 pastry rings for the gâteaux: roll out the puff pastry dough to a 26' X 18 inch rectangle and cut six 8–9 inch rounds. Cut out the centers of each round with the 5–6 inch lid as a guide, making 6 large rings and 6 rounds of dough. Roll out each round until 8–9 inches in diameter and cut out six more 5–6 inch rounds. Put 2 of the 5–6 inch rounds together and roll them out thinly to 8–9 inches diameter to make a base; do the same with the 2 remaining pairs.

Place the 12 pastry rings a few at a time on the baking sheets, prick them well with a fork and bake in heated oven for 8–10 minutes or until

brown. Place the 3 pastry bases on the dampened baking sheets, prick them with a fork and bake 12–15 minutes or until brown.

Cut the pastry trimmings into tiny stars, diamonds and half moons, and place them on a dampened baking sheet and bake 5–7 minutes. Cool all the pastry.

To make the lemon curd filling: put all the ingredients in the top of a double boiler (not metal). Cook over hot water for 10–15 minutes, stirring gently until the lemon curd is thick but still falls easily from the spoon. The water must not boil or the mixture will separate. Pour it into a bowl and cool.

Brush the cool pastry with apricot jam glaze and place 4 rings (one on top of another) on each pastry base. Brush the top and sides of each gâteau with apricot jam glaze and decorate the top with small pastry shapes, pieces of candied fruit or nuts.

Not more than 1 hour before serving, whip the cream until it starts to thicken, then fold two-thirds into the cool lemon curd. Spoon one-third of the filling into the cavity of each gâteau; using a pastry bag fitted with a star tube, decorate the gâteaux with rosettes of reserved cream, whipped until stiff. Sprinkle chopped candied fruit or chopped nuts on top of the cream.

Apricot Jam Glaze

The glaze keeps well, so make 2 cups or more at a time to use as needed. Store in a covered jar.

In a saucepan bring slowly to a boil 12 oz of apricot jam with the juice of ½ lemon and 2 tablespoons water. Stir until smooth, simmer 5 minutes, strain and return to the pan. Boil 5 minutes more and pour into a jar for storage.

Fruit Compote

6 bananas, peeled
1 can (15¾ oz) pineapple
   chunks
1 can (16 oz) apricots
1 can (16 oz) peach slices
6 oranges, peeled and cut in
   sections
2 lb seedless green grapes
½ cup kirsch, brandy or Grand
   Marnier (optional)

Method
Cut the bananas in diagonal slices and pour over the juice from the cans of fruit. Add the orange sections and the grapes. Put in the canned fruit, spoon over the liqueur, if used, and mix the fruits well. Cover and chill.

HOW TO MAKE PASTRY (4) PUFF

Puff pastry is one of the great inventions of French cuisine. The ideal crisp airy puff pastry has a melting flavor of butter and rises in the oven 3–4 times the height of the original dough. The pastry rises because it is made of innumerable thicknesses of dough layered with butter. If the layers of dough are uneven the pastry is lopsided, and if the layers stick together it will not rise at all.

The best known puff pastry dishes are bouchées, vol-au-vents and mille feuilles, although the dough can be used in many other ways. A vol-au-vent (puff of wind) is a pastry case usually 6–7 inches in diameter that rises 2–3 inches or more during baking. Once baked, a circle is removed from the top to form a lid and some of the soft, uncooked pastry from the center is scooped out. Just before serving, the vol-au-vent is filled with a rich mixture of shellfish, meat or chicken, bound with a béchamel, velouté or any white sauce. A bouchée (mouthful) is similar to a vol-au-vent but is smaller. Individual bouchées served as an entrée or appetizer are about $2\frac{1}{4}$ inches in diameter; for cocktail hors d'œuvre, they should be $1-1\frac{1}{2}$ inches in diameter. The same savory fillings can be used as for vol-au-vents.

A puff pastry flan case is like a vol-au-vent but it is shallower and larger in diameter. When baked it can be filled with a savory mixture as for a vol-au-vent or with fresh fruit and then covered with a glaze.

A mille feuilles, or Napoleon, is a rich melting pastry made of thin layers of puff pastry sandwiched with whipped cream or a flavored filling.

Perfect light puff pastry is not hard to make if you follow the rules, but it is wiser to start with simple recipes like mille feuilles and jalousies and then go on to bouchées and vol-au-vents when you are sure of your skill.

Favorite dishes made with puff pastry are whole mille feuilles (at front), fresh fruit flan and jalousie (recipes on pages 76 and 81)

Points to remember

1 Everything must be cool: ingredients, mixing bowl, pastry board, rolling pin and, most important of all, your hands. Marble is the ideal working surface as it is cool, but a Formica-type surface is adequate. If possible make puff pastry before the kitchen is warm and steamy from other cooking. Never try to make it in hot weather without air conditioning.

2 The consistency of the foundation dough is vital; if not correct, begin again rather than waste butter.

3 Roll out the dough correctly; the pressure on the rolling pin must be firm and in a downwards motion. Roll only in one direction to make sure the pressure is even.

4 It is important to remove any leftover pieces of dough from the work surface after each rolling. If you don't clean the surface thoroughly, the next time you roll out the dough it may pick up the pieces and become lumpy.

5 It is essential to preheat the oven to the correct temperature when baking pastry.

To form the dough

For perfect puff pastry, the butter and flour must be correctly prepared and the water for mixing must be ice cold. Butter is used for its flavor and texture — it should be lightly salted and of the best quality.

To make butter the right consistency for rolling, it must be worked until pliable: lightly flour the butter and place it between 2 sheets of wax paper, pound it with a rolling pin until flat, lift off the top sheet of wax paper, fold the butter in half, replace the wax paper and continue to pound and fold until the butter is pliable but not sticky. Shape it into a 5 inch square, dust lightly with flour, wrap and chill until firm but not hard.

Use all-purpose flour and sift thoroughly. For foundation dough, work a little butter into the flour, add two-thirds of the water with the lemon juice and stir until a dough begins to form. Add most of the remaining water at once — if it is added a little at a time it will dry in the flour and the dough will be tough. However, reserve a little water as some flours need less water than others.

The finished dough should be firm yet pliable and have the same consistency as the butter although the textures are different.

Knead the dough firmly for 1–2 minutes – this, with the lemon juice, develops the gluten in the flour so the dough doesn't crack when rolled and folded. Let dough stand 15 minutes to 'relax' and lose elasticity.

To enclose the butter

On a lightly floured board, roll out the foundation dough to a 12 inch square – the dough will be hard to roll as it is firm, but it should not be elastic.

Lay the square of butter in the center of the dough and fold the dough around it like a parcel. Seal the parcel by pressing the edges firmly with a rolling pin, cover the dough and chill 15 minutes.

To roll out the dough

Bring the rolling pin down sharply onto the dough 3–4 times to flatten it slightly, then roll it away from you with a strong firm downward pressure. Avoid pushing the dough, as this stretches it.

To keep the dough straight, apply an even pressure on both sides – many people have a tendency to put more weight on the right or left hand, which pulls the dough to one side – and use short strokes.

Lift the rolling pin at the end of a stroke, then bring it down at the point to which it was last rolled and continue rolling forward in one direction. Continue until just before you reach the edge of the dough.

Watchpoint: never let the rolling pin run off the edge of the dough as the idea is to keep the dough to a strict rectangular shape.

The whole area of dough should be rolled in an even layer $\frac{1}{2}$–$\frac{3}{4}$ inch thick and 5–6 inches wide – it should be almost 3 times as long as it is

Fold up the basic dough like a parcel around square of butter

Roll out the dough to a large rectangle and fold it in three

wide.

Graduate the thickness of the rolling so the dough gets thinner and the rectangle gets progressively larger as it nears completion. If it is rolled thinly at the beginning, the butter may break through.

Watchpoint: do not turn the dough over; it should only be rolled on one side.

Each rolling and folding is called a 'turn' and puff pastry is usually given 6 turns and chilled for 15 minutes after every 2 turns. This rest removes any elasticity from the dough and chilling makes it easier to work.

At the end of each turn, fold the dough in three (as

Turn the folded dough so the open ends face towards you

Press rolling pin down evenly to flatten dough and seal edges

shown in the photographs, above), seal the edges with the rolling pin to prevent the folds from shifting when the dough is rolled out and half turn the dough (see basic recipe) so the open ends face towards you; this way it is rolled in a different direction each time.

Watchpoint: if at any stage the butter starts to break through the dough, stop rolling at once, sprinkle the dough with flour, and chill it thoroughly for 15–30 minutes before continuing.

If the dough is streaky at the end of 6 turns, it means the butter has not been rolled in completely, so give it

another turn.

When completed, chill the dough for 15 minutes, roll it out and cut it to the required shape. Or it can be wrapped in a plastic bag and stored in the refrigerator for 1–2 days if you like.

Watchpoint: when cutting puff pastry for shapes that must rise evenly, like vol-au-vents, bouchées and flan cases, do not use dough within $\frac{1}{2}$ inch of the edge because the layers are uneven.

Save all the trimmings and fold them in three. Place them all on top of each other, roll out and use them for making mille feuilles, palmiers, jalousies or sacristans (see pages 81–83), or other small puff pastries.

To bake puff pastry

After shaping, place the dough on a baking sheet and chill in refrigerator for about 15 minutes or until firm (but not more than 30 minutes).

The baking sheet should be dampened with cold water. This helps to prevent the pastry from sliding and shrinking too much while baking.

Watchpoint: use a thick baking sheet so it does not bend in the heat from the oven, making the pastry rise unevenly.

Bake puff pastry in a hot oven (425°F). A large vol-au-vent should be baked in the center of the oven but small shapes like bouchées should be baked about 5 inches from the top of the oven or where it is the hottest. For the most accurate information about heat distribution, consult the manufacturer's handbook.

Egg Glaze
To make egg glaze: beat 1 egg with $\frac{1}{2}$ teaspoon salt; the salt liquefies the egg, so it is easy to brush a thin film on the dough and it also increases the shine when baked.

Egg glaze acts as a seal, so do not let it touch the cut edge of puff or flaky dough as this will prevent the pastry from rising.

Basic Puff Pastry

2 cups flour
1 cup butter
pinch of salt
1 teaspoon lemon juice
$\frac{1}{2}$–$\frac{3}{4}$ cup ice water

This quantity of pastry makes a vol-au-vent for 4 people or 15–18 medium bouchées. Use the leftover trimmings for the recipes on pages 81–83.

Method
Reserve 1 tablespoon of butter and place the rest, lightly floured, between 2 pieces of wax paper. Pound with a rolling pin, remove the top piece of wax paper, fold the butter in half, replace the wax paper and pound again. Continue in this way until the butter is pliable but not sticky. Shape it into a 5 inch square, dust lightly with flour and chill until firm but not hard.

Sift the flour and salt into a bowl or onto a marble slab and rub in the reserved 1 tablespoon butter. Add the lemon juice to $\frac{1}{2}$ cup of the water.

Make a well in the center of the flour and pour in the water and lemon juice. Mix with a spatula or round-bladed knife in the bowl or use your fingers on a marble slab. When a dough begins to form, add most of the remaining water. Mix to a firm, pliable dough, adding the remaining water if necessary.

Lightly dust a marble slab or work surface with flour and knead the dough for 1–2 minutes. Let stand 15 minutes, then roll out to a 12 inch square.

Place the butter in the center of the dough and fold it over the butter, wrapping the sides and ends over like a parcel. Wrap in plastic wrap or a plastic bag and chill 15 minutes.

Sprinkle the work surface lightly with flour, put down the dough with the joins facing up, and bring the rolling pin firmly down on the dough 3–4 times to flatten it slightly.

Roll out to a rectangle about 5–6 inches wide and almost 3 times as long. Fold it into three, one end over the other, as accurately as possible; if necessary pull the corners to keep them in a rectangle. Seal the edges with the rolling pin and turn the dough half around to bring the open edges towards you. Roll out again and fold in three.

Keep a note of the 'turns' made by marking the dough lightly with the appropriate number of fingerprints. Wrap and chill 15 minutes.

Repeat this process, giving the dough 6 turns altogether with a 15 minute rest after every 2 turns. Wrap and refrigerate until needed.

Vol-au-vent and Bouchée Cases

The larger the case, the thicker the dough must be rolled.

A vol-au-vent of 6–7 inches diameter should be made from a $\frac{3}{4}$–1 inch thickness of dough.

A bouchée of $1\frac{1}{2}$–2 inches in diameter needs only three-eighth inch thickness of dough.

If pastry is too thick for the size of bouchée, it will topple over in the oven when it has risen to a certain height.

Puff pastry always shrinks in diameter during baking, so use a cutter one size larger than you want the finished bouchée to be. For example, a $2\frac{1}{2}$ inch round of uncooked dough makes a 2–$2\frac{1}{4}$ inch bouchée.

Vol-au-vent

2 cup quantity of puff pastry, well chilled
egg glaze

6–7 inch pan lid; 3–4 inch plain cookie cutter or pan lid

Method
Set oven at hot (425°F).

Roll out the prepared pastry dough on a lightly floured marble slab or work surface to an 8–9 inch square, $\frac{3}{4}$–1 inch thick.

To cut a vol-au-vent shape: place 6–7 inch pan lid on dough and cut around it with a knife; hold the knife slanting to form a sloping edge – wider at the base. Cut with a sawing motion so the dough is severed cleanly. Turn the round of dough upside down and set on a dampened baking sheet so that the widest part is on top. Brush lightly with egg glaze, making sure that none drips down the sides.

With the cutter or small pan lid, mark a circle in the center of the round of dough.

With the tip of a knife, blunt side down, mark outer ring of vol-au-vent with V's and inner circle with a diamond pattern (see photographs).

To help the dough rise, mark the sides of the vol-au-vent by placing the side of the left forefinger on top of the edge of the dough and, with the back of a knife, make horizontal indentations all around. If you like, scallop the edges by holding the knife vertically and, at $\frac{1}{2}$ inch intervals, pull the knife gently towards the center of the vol-au-vent to make a $\frac{1}{4}$ inch deep indentation.

Chill the dough 10–15 minutes, then bake in heated oven for 25–30 minutes or until the vol-au-vent is puffed and brown.

Slide onto a rack to cool and, while still warm, cut around the inner circle with the point of a knife to remove the 'lid'. Set this aside and carefully scoop out most of the soft center.

Place the vol-au-vent case on a platter before filling it. It can be baked ahead of time and reheated, but do not add filling until just before serving.

Vol-au-vents can be filled with shellfish, veal, chicken, sweetbreads, kidneys or mushrooms, bound with a béchamel, velouté, or any white sauce (see recipes here and in Volume 2).

Shape a vol-au-vent by cutting around the pan lid placed on the rolled out dough

Using the blunt side of knife, decorate with V's around edge and diamond pattern in center

When baked, remove center circle or lid of vol-au-vent and scoop out the soft center

A vol-au-vent and two bouchées — one entrée size and a smaller one to be served with cocktails — are filled with savory mixtures

Bouchées

2 cup quantity of puff pastry,
   well chilled
egg glaze (see page 74)

2½ inch fluted cookie cutter;
   1½ inch cutter, fluted or plain

Makes 15—18 bouchées.

Method

Set oven at hot (425°F).

Roll out the prepared pastry dough to three-eighth inch thickness and brush with egg glaze.

To cut bouchées: stamp out rounds with the large fluted cutter, keeping them close together so that no dough is wasted but leaving about ¾ inch border around the edge. As the rounds are cut, lift them onto a dampened baking sheet.

With the smaller cookie cutter, make a circular mark in the center of each one, cutting down a little into the dough.

Chill the bouchées for 15 minutes, then bake in heated oven for 15—20 minutes or until they are puffed and golden brown. Lift them onto a wire rack to cool.

While still warm lift out the center 'lid' with the point of a knife and scoop out any soft center with a teaspoon.

Just before serving, reheat the bouchées and spoon in a hot filling.

If bouchées are very small, split them (instead of cutting out the center 'lid') and then fill with a teaspoon of filling.

Flan Case

2 cup quantity of puff pastry,
   well chilled
egg glaze (see page 74)

2 pan lids or flan rings
   (8 and 6 inches diameter)

Method

Set oven at hot (425°F).

Roll out the prepared pastry dough to ½ inch thickness.

To cut a flan case: place the large pan lid or flan ring on the dough and cut around it with a knife, keeping the knife vertical. Place the smaller lid or ring, on this round of dough and cut out a center round. You will now have an outer ring, 1 inch wide, and a 6 inch diameter round.

Slide the outer ring to one side and pile the trimmings on the 6 inch round. Roll this to make a larger but thinner round 8 inches in diameter and about ¼ inch thick for the flan base.

Lift this round onto a dampened baking sheet and brush it lightly with egg glaze (do not let any drip down the sides). Lift the ring onto it and adjust both layers so they make one neat round.

With a finger, gently press the center of the ring all the way around so that it sticks firmly to the round underneath.

To help the dough rise, mark the sides of the flan by placing the side of your left forefinger on top of the edge of the dough and, with the back of a knife, make horizontal indentations all around. If you like, scallop the edges by holding the knife vertically and, at ½ inch intervals, pull the knife gently towards the center of the flan to make ¼ inch deep indentations.

Brush the top of the ring

with egg glaze and mark with the back of a knife in V patterns to decorate.

Prick the center of the round with a fork, chill 15 minutes and bake in heated oven for 25—30 minutes or until the flan is puffed and brown. Cool slightly, then slide onto a wire rack to cool completely.

Fill with a savory or sweet filling, such as apricot, mushroom or shrimp, as for flans made of pie pastry (see Volume 3).

To cut a flan case, place large flan ring on pastry dough and cut around it, keeping the knife vertical. Place smaller flan ring on this round of dough; cut out a center round to give 2 rings of dough

Shrimp and Egg Bouchées

2 cup quantity of puff pastry,
   well chilled
egg glaze (see page 74)

For filling
½ lb peeled, cooked shrimps,
   coarsely chopped
2 hard-cooked eggs, finely
   chopped
1½ cups béchamel sauce, made
   with 2 tablespoons butter,

2 tablespoons flour, and 1½
   cups milk (infused with a
   slice of onion, ½ bay leaf,
   blade of mace, 6 peppercorns)
salt and pepper
2 tablespoons heavy cream
   (optional)

2½ and 1½ inch cookie cutters,
   fluted or plain

Makes 15—18 bouchées.

Method

Set oven at hot (425°F).

Roll out the prepared pastry dough, cut, glaze and bake the bouchées in heated oven for 15—20 minutes or until puffed and golden.

To make the filling: make the béchamel sauce, season and simmer 2 minutes. Stir in the shrimps and chopped eggs with the cream, if used, and season to taste.

Remove the lids from the bouchées, scoop out any soft center and fill with the egg and shrimp mixture. Replace the lids on a slant, reheat a few minutes in a moderate oven (350°F) and serve.

Kidney and Mushroom Bouchées

2 cup quantity of puff pastry,
   well chilled
egg glaze (see page 74)

For filling
1 lb lamb or veal kidneys
2 cups (½ lb) small mushrooms,
   quartered
2 tablespoons butter
1 onion, finely chopped
1 tablespoon flour
¼ cup Marsala or sherry
1 cup stock
bouquet garni
salt and pepper
¼ cup heavy cream
box of small cress (for garnish)
   —optional

Kidney and mushroom bouchées are served on a bed of small cress

**2½ and 1½ inch cookie cutters
fluted or plain**

Method

Set oven at hot (425°F).

Roll out the pastry dough, cut out bouchées, glaze and bake them in heated oven for 15—20 minutes or until they are puffed and golden.

To make the filling: remove the skin from the kidneys, if necessary, and cut out the cores with scissors. Cut kidneys in ¾ inch pieces.

In a skillet melt the butter and fry the kidneys quickly until they are just browned. Remove them, add the onion and cook until soft but not browned. Stir in the flour and cook 1 minute or until

lightly browned. Put back the kidneys, add the Marsala or sherry and flame.

Add the stock, bouquet garni and seasoning, cover and simmer 25—30 minutes or until the kidneys are tender. Add the mushrooms and cook 5 minutes longer. Discard the bouquet garni, stir in the cream and taste the sauce for seasoning.

Remove the pastry lids from the bouchées, scoop out the soft center and fill with the kidney and mushroom mixture. Replace the lids on top, at a slant, reheat bouchées for a few minutes until hot and serve them on a bed of small cress, if you like.

Sweetbread Vol-au-vent

2 cup quantity of puff pastry, well chilled
egg glaze (see page 74)

For filling
2–3 pairs (1½ lb) calves' sweetbreads
large pinch of salt
2 slices of lemon
bouquet garni
1 small onion, quartered
1½–2 cups stock or water
1 tablespoon butter
1 cup (¼ lb) small mushrooms

For sauce
2 tablespoons butter
2 tablespoons flour
¾ cup light cream
salt and pepper
1 egg yolk
2 teaspoons chopped parsley
squeeze of lemon juice

Method

Soak the sweetbreads for 3–5 hours in cold water with 1 slice of lemon or a few drops of vinegar. Drain, rinse and put them in a pan, cover with cold water and add salt and another slice of lemon. Bring to a boil over low heat, skimming the top when necessary.

Drain and rinse the sweetbreads quickly in cold water. Drain again, and remove any ducts or skin that will pull off easily. Press between two plates with a 2 lb weight on top and leave until cold.

Put the sweetbreads in a pan with the bouquet garni, onion and enough stock or water to cover. Simmer 15 minutes or until the sweetbreads are tender. Drain. Strain the stock, boil it until reduced to ¾ cup and reserve.

Melt the tablespoon of butter and sauté the mushrooms until soft.

Set the oven at hot (425°F).

Roll out the pastry dough,

cut the vol-au-vent, brush with egg glaze and bake in heated oven for 25–30 minutes or until puffed and brown. While still warm, remove the lid and scoop out the soft center.

To make the sauce: melt the butter, stir in the flour off the heat and pour on the stock from the sweetbreads with the cream, reserving 2 tablespoons. Bring to a boil, stirring, simmer 3 minutes and season.

Mix the reserved cream with the egg yolk, add a little of the hot sauce and blend this into the remaining sauce, off the heat. Stir in the parsley and lemon juice. Add the sweetbreads with the mushrooms, shake the pan gently to mix and reheat without boiling. Adjust seasoning.

Just before serving, reheat the vol-au-vent in a moderate oven (350°F) for 8–10 minutes. Set on a platter and fill with the sweetbread mixture. Replace the lid on a slant and serve.

Vol-au-vent aux Fruits de Mer (Seafood Vol-au-vent)

2 cup quantity of puff pastry, well chilled
egg glaze (see page 74)

For filling
½ lb bay or sea scallops
½ lb cooked lobster meat
½ lb cooked, peeled medium shrimps
½ cup white wine
½ cup fish stock or water
1 cup (¼ lb) mushrooms, quartered
squeeze of lemon juice
½ teaspoon butter
2 tablespoons water
salt and pepper

For sauce
2 tablespoons butter
2 tablespoons flour
¾ cup light cream
2 egg yolks

Method

Set oven at hot (425°F).

Roll out the pastry dough, cut out the vol-au-vent, brush it with glaze and bake in heated oven for 25–30 minutes or until it is puffed and brown. While it is still warm, remove the lid and scoop out the soft center. Transfer to a wire rack to cool.

To make the filling: poach the scallops in the wine and fish stock or water, allowing 2–3 minutes for bay scallops and 4–5 minutes for sea scallops. Drain them, reserving the scallops, and boil the cooking liquid until it is reduced to ¾ cup.

Put the mushrooms in a pan with the lemon juice, butter, 2 tablespoons water, salt and pepper, cover and cook over high heat for 1–2 minutes or until they are just tender.

To make the sauce: in a saucepan melt the butter, stir

in the flour and pour in the reduced scallop liquid. Add the liquid from cooking the mushrooms and bring to a boil, stirring until the sauce thickens. Season, stir in ½ cup cream, add the scallops, lobster meat, shrimps and mushrooms, cover and heat gently until very hot.

Just before serving, reheat the vol-au-vent and set it on a platter. Stir the remaining cream into the egg yolks, add a little of the hot seafood mixture and stir this liaison back into the remaining mixture. Heat the sauce until it thickens slightly but do not boil. Taste for seasoning, pile the filling into the vol-au-vent and set the lid on top, at a slant.

Fruit Turnovers

1½ cup quantity of puff pastry
    trimmings, well chilled
¾ cup strawberry, apricot or
    raspberry jam
1 egg white, beaten until frothy
granulated sugar (for
    sprinkling)

4 inch cookie cutter

Makes 10–12 turnovers.

Method
Set oven at hot (425°F).
    Roll out the pastry dough very thinly and cut out rounds with the cookie cutter. Put a spoonful of jam in the center of each round and brush the edges with water. Fold over to form turnovers and press the edges together firmly. Slash the top with scissors or a knife so steam can escape; chill the turnovers for 10–15 minutes.

    Bake the turnovers in heated oven for 15–20 minutes or until they are puffed and brown. Five minutes before the end of cooking, brush the turnovers with beaten egg white, sprinkle generously with sugar and continue baking.

    Serve the turnovers hot or transfer them to a wire rack to cool.

Fruit turnovers, sprinkled with sugar, are delicious puff pastries

Use puff pastry trimmings for many pastries such as (from left): sacristans and mille feuilles, jalousies and palmiers

Mille Feuilles
(Napoleons)

$1\frac{1}{2}$ cup quantity of puff pastry
  or trimmings, well chilled
$\frac{1}{4}$ cup raspberry jam
1 cup heavy cream, whipped
  until it holds a soft shape

For icing
1 cup confectioners' sugar
2 tablespoons water or
  2 tablespoons sugar syrup
  (made with 2 tablespoons
  sugar dissolved in $\frac{1}{4}$ cup
  water, then boiled until
  reduced to 2 tablespoons)
$\frac{1}{2}$ teaspoon vanilla

Method
Set oven at hot (425°F).

Roll out the prepared pastry dough as thinly as possible to a large rectangle. Lay this on a dampened baking sheet, letting the dough come slightly over the edge. Prick the dough well all over with a fork and chill 10 minutes.

Bake the dough in heated oven for 10–15 minutes or until brown. Loosen the pastry with a spatula and turn it over. Bake 5 minutes longer, then transfer to a wire rack to cool.

When cold, trim the edges and cut the remaining pastry into 3 strips, each about 3 inches wide. Crush the trimmings lightly.

Spread two strips of pastry with raspberry jam. Spread half the whipped cream on one strip, place the other on top, press down lightly and spread with the remaining cream. Top with the last strip of pastry and press down again. Press the layers together to prevent them from slipping when sliced.

To make the icing: mix the confectioners' sugar until smooth with enough water or sugar syrup to make an icing that spreads easily. Add the vanilla. Warm the icing to tepid – it should coat the back of a spoon but, if it is too thick, add more liquid.

Spread the icing quickly on top of the mille feuilles and at once press the crushed trimmings around the edges to decorate. Cut in $1\frac{1}{2}$–2 inch slices to serve.

Watchpoint: mille feuilles pastry must be thoroughly baked so it is a deep brown and very crisp.

Carefully spread the layers of pastry for mille feuilles (literally – a thousand leaves) with jam and whipped cream

Jalousie

$1\frac{1}{2}$ cup quantity of puff pastry,
  or trimmings, well chilled
5–6 tablespoons strawberry,
  apricot or plum jam, or
  apple marmelade purée
1 egg white, beaten until frothy
granulated sugar (for
  sprinkling)

This dessert is called jalousie because it resembles a shutter with movable louvres that is called a 'jalousie' in France.

Method
Set oven at hot (425°F).

Roll out the prepared pastry dough to a large rectangle $\frac{1}{4}$ inch thick and cut out a 10 X 4 inch piece. Fold this piece in half lengthwise and, with a sharp knife, cut across the fold at $\frac{1}{4}$ inch intervals to within $\frac{1}{2}$ inch of the outer edge.

Fold the trimmings and roll out thinly to another 10 X 4 inch rectangle and lift onto a dampened baking sheet.

Spoon the jam or marmelade purée down the center of the dough and spread it to within 1 inch of the edge. Brush the edges with cold water, then lift the first rectangle on top with the folded edge in the center. Open out the folded dough and press the edge down onto the lower piece. Cut around the edges to neaten and chill 10 minutes.

Bake jalousie in heated oven for 25–30 minutes. About 5–10 minutes before the end of baking, take the jalousie from the oven, brush it with egg white and sprinkle generously with sugar. Replace in the oven and continue baking until golden brown.

Serve the jalousie hot or slide it onto a rack to cool and serve cold. Cut in 2–$2\frac{1}{2}$ inch slices before serving.

Marmelade Purée

Wash tart apples, wipe, quarter and core them. Thickly butter a heavy flameproof casserole and put the apples into the pot. Add a strip of lemon rind, cover with a piece of buttered brown paper and a lid and cook gently until soft, stirring occasionally. Remove the lemon rind and purée the apples in a blender or work through a nylon sieve.

Rinse out the pot, return the purée to it and add 3–4 tablespoons sugar per cup of purée or to taste. Cook rapidly on top of the stove, stirring constantly, or bake in a moderately hot oven (375°F) until the mixture is stiff but still falls easily from a spoon.

When cold, this marmelade sets firmly. Use to fill pies, flans and cakes or a jalousie.

Palmiers can also be sandwiched with whipped cream

Palmiers

1½ cup quantity of puff pastry, or trimmings, well chilled
granulated sugar (for sprinkling)
heavy cream, stiffly whipped (to serve) – optional

Method

Roll out the prepared pastry dough to a rectangle. Sprinkle generously with sugar, fold in three (one end over the other) and roll out again. Sprinkle again with sugar, fold in three, and roll out. Fold in three again and chill 15 minutes.

Set oven at hot (425°F).

Roll out the dough to a 10 inch square about ¼ inch thick. Fold the edge nearest to you over twice to reach the center of the dough; repeat this from the other side. Press lightly with a rolling pin and fold one rolled section of dough on top of the other. Press again.

With a sharp knife cut across the dough into ½ inch wide slices. Lay these, cut side down, on a dampened baking sheet, leaving room for them to spread. Open the slices slightly and flatten with the heel of your hand to a palm leaf shape (as in photograph opposite).

Bake palmiers in heated oven for 10–12 minutes. When beginning to brown, turn the palmiers over so that both sides will caramelize. When brown and sticky, lift onto a wire rack to cool.

Serve palmiers plain or sandwiched with whipped cream.

Sacristans

1 cup quantity of puff pastry or trimmings, well chilled
1 egg, beaten to mix
½ cup whole blanched almonds, finely chopped
granulated sugar (for sprinkling)

Method

Set oven at hot (425°F).

Roll out the prepared pastry dough to a thin strip 5 inches wide. Brush with beaten egg, leaving a ½ inch border at each side. Sprinkle with chopped almonds, pressing them down lightly so they stick, and sprinkle generously with the granulated sugar.

Cut the dough into strips about ¾ inch wide, twist them several times and lay on a dampened baking sheet. Press down each end firmly and bake in heated oven for 8–10 minutes or until browned. Carefully lift the pastries from the baking sheet and cool them on a wire rack.

Raspberry Feuilletées

2 cup quantity of puff pastry, well chilled
egg glaze (see page 74)

For filling
1 quart fresh raspberries
½ cup red currant jelly glaze
Chantilly cream, made with
    ½ cup heavy cream, stiffly whipped and flavored with
    ½ teaspoon vanilla and
    1–2 teaspoons sugar

Pastry bag and medium star tube

Small fresh strawberries, blueberries or pitted cherries may be substituted for the raspberries. Makes 6 feuilletées.

Method

Roll out the pastry dough to a 5 X 15 inch rectangle and brush with egg glaze. Trim the edges, cut the dough crosswise into 6 rectangles and set them on a dampened baking sheet.

With a small knife, mark a lid ¼ inch inside the edge of each rectangle, cutting a little way into the dough but not through it. With the back of a knife, mark a lattice pattern on the lids to decorate. Chill the rectangles for 15 minutes.

Bake the feuilletées in the heated oven for 15–20 minutes or until they are puffed and brown. Transfer them to a wire rack to cool. While still warm, remove the lids with the point of a knife and scoop out any soft center with a teaspoon.

A short time before serving, pile the raspberries in the feuilletées and brush them with melted red currant jelly glaze. Decorate the tops of the raspberries with rosettes of whipped Chantilly cream, using a pastry bag fitted with the star tube. Place the lids on top, at a slant.

Apple Galette

1 cup quantity of puff pastry trimmings, well chilled
egg glaze (see page 74)
1 tablespoon chopped mint (for sprinkling)

For filling
5–6 Golden Delicious or other dessert apples, pared, cored and cut in chunks
¼ cup sugar, or to taste
¼ cup water
grated rind and juice of ½ lemon
2–3 sprigs of fresh mint

Method

Set oven at hot (425°F).

Divide the pastry dough in half and roll out to two 9 inch rounds. Trim the pastry edges and transfer the rounds to dampened baking sheets. Prick the dough well all over with a fork. Brush with egg glaze and mark 1 round with the back of a knife in a lattice pattern or other decoration. Chill 15 minutes.

Bake the rounds in heated oven for 10–15 minutes or until they are brown. Transfer them to a wire rack to cool.

To make the filling: put the apples in a saucepan with the sugar, water, lemon rind and juice and mint sprigs. Cover and cook gently, stirring occasionally, for 10–15minutes or until the apples are pulpy but not soft enough to purée. Discard the mint leaves, add more sugar to taste if necessary and let cool.

A short time before serving, set the undecorated pastry round on a platter and spread with the apple mixture. Top with the decorated pastry round and sprinkle with chopped mint.

HOW TO MAKE CHRISTMAS PUDDING AND MINCEMEAT

Few festive desserts can match the glamour of the traditional Christmas plum pudding, carried flaming from the kitchen and topped with a sprig of holly. Mince pies are less spectacular but even richer in flavor and homemade mincemeat bears little resemblance to the commercial fruit mixture of the same name — good mincemeat is enriched with suet and laced with plenty of liquor.

Christmas puddings and mincemeat are easy to make at home and the only chore is preparing the fruit and nuts. Then it is simply a matter of combining the ingredients in the largest possible bowl.

Mincemeat is stored, uncooked, in a large crock or jar, but Christmas puddings must be cooked in boiling water for several hours before storing.

Like fruit cakes the flavor of Christmas puddings and mincemeat develops when stored for 1–2 months so make them well ahead of time and keep them, covered, in a dry place; refrigeration, however, is not necessary.

Preparation of Ingredients

Fruit: pick over currants and raisins to remove any stalks.

Almonds: to blanch, pour boiling water over the shelled nuts in a bowl and leave to cool. Pinch the ends and the skins will slip off easily. Rinse and dry thoroughly. To sliver almonds, blanch, skin and split them in two; cut each half lengthwise into slivers.

Candied peel: the best peel is sold in 'caps' because it retains more moisture and flavor. Remove any sugar from the peel, soak it in warm water if it is very hard and chop it finely. If using already chopped peel, be sure it is not dry.

Suet: butchers will supply suet and grind it for you. The best suet comes from around the beef kidney as it contains very little membrane.

Christmas Puddings

Traditionally every member of the household would stir the Christmas plum pudding for luck. Small silver charms were added to the mixture — a bachelor's button, spinster's thimble, rich man's coin, poor man's bean; the recipient at the Christmas table then knew his — or her — fortune for the coming year.

Rich Christmas Pudding

2 cups self-rising flour
1 teaspoon salt
1 teaspoon ground nutmeg
$\frac{1}{2}$ teaspoon ground allspice
$\frac{1}{2}$ teaspoon ground cinnamon
$\frac{1}{4}$ teaspoon ground cloves
4 cups fresh white breadcrumbs
1$\frac{1}{2}$ cups ($\frac{3}{4}$ lb) ground beef suet
2 cups dark brown sugar
3 cups currants
3 cups golden raisins
6 cups raisins
1 cup chopped mixed candied peel
$\frac{1}{4}$ cup whole blanched almonds, slivered
1 large tart apple, pared, cored and grated
grated rind and juice of 1 orange
6 eggs
$\frac{3}{4}$ cup milk or ale

4 heatproof bowls (1$\frac{1}{2}$ quart capacity each), or 2 bowls (3 quart capacity each)

Method
Thoroughly grease the bowls; have a fish kettle or enough large saucepans of boiling water to hold the bowls ready.
Sift the flour with the salt and spices into a very large mixing bowl. Add the breadcrumbs, suet, sugar, dried fruit, almonds, grated apple and orange rind and mix well together. Make a well in the center.

Beat the eggs until frothy, add the orange juice and milk or ale and pour into the well. Stir until the pudding is thoroughly mixed, then fill the prepared bowls up to the top.

To cover the bowls, butter a large round of brown paper for each one, cut a piece of foil the same size and put both rounds together, foil up. Make a 1 inch pleat across the center (this allows for expansion) and lay over the bowls, buttered side down. Tie securely with string, leaving a loop for easy removal when cooked.

Place the bowls in the fish kettle or saucepans with enough boiling water to cover. Cook large puddings for 7 hours and smaller ones for 5 hours. Boil them steadily, adding more boiling water as it evaporates.
Note: it is important that the puddings should boil continuously.

When cooked, lift the bowls out carefully and cool. Remove the foil and brown paper, replace with freshly buttered brown paper and foil and store in a dry place.

When ready to serve at Christmas, boil or steam the puddings 1 hour longer and turn out onto a hot platter. Serve brandy or rum hard sauce separately (recipes are given on page 89).

Christmas Pudding

2 cups flour
$\frac{1}{2}$ teaspoon salt
3 cups fresh white breadcrumbs
1$\frac{1}{2}$ cups ground beef suet
1 cup sugar
1$\frac{1}{2}$ cups currants
1$\frac{1}{2}$ cups golden raisins
1$\frac{1}{2}$ cups raisins
$\frac{1}{2}$ cup chopped candied peel
$\frac{1}{2}$ cup grated raw carrot
1 tablespoon molasses
1 cup milk

4 heatproof bowls (1 quart capacity each), or 3 bowls (1$\frac{1}{2}$ quart capacity each)

Method
Mix, cook and store as for rich Christmas pudding, allowing 4 hours boiling for the small puddings or 5 hours for the larger ones.

Leftover Christmas Pudding

Leftover Christmas pudding is delicious if cut in slices, fried in butter until very hot and served with hard sauce or sprinkled with confectioners' sugar. Alternatively, freeze it, then cut in very thin slices and serve with vanilla ice cream.

Sugar and spice, fruit and nuts, fat and eggs, milk or ale — all combine to make a rich Christmas pudding

Serve Christmas pudding in traditional style — flaming and topped with a holly sprig

Mince Pies

Mincemeat used to be made of minced meat with spices, fruit and liquor; it was originally invented as a way to preserve valuable meat through the long winter months. Although other methods of preserving are now used and most mincemeat no longer contains any meat, it is still popular in various forms.

Traditional Mincemeat

2 cups ground beef suet
3 cups cooked ground lean beef
2 cups raisins

2 cups currants
2 cups chopped mixed candied peel
2 cups pared, cored and chopped tart apples
grated rind of 3 lemons
grated rind of 3 oranges
2 cups brown sugar
1 teaspoon ground nutmeg
1 teaspoon ground cloves
1 teaspoon ground cinnamon
1 teaspoon ground allspice
1½ cups Madeira, sherry or port
1½ cups brandy

Makes about 15 cups.

Method
Combine all the ingredients except the wine and brandy and mix very thoroughly. Pour over the wine and brandy and mix again.

Pack the mixture into glass jars or crocks and cover with tight-fitting lids or with several layers of plastic wrap tied down firmly with string.

When carefully sealed to prevent evaporation, the mincemeat will keep almost indefinitely in a dry place.

Simple Mincemeat

2 cups ground beef suet
3 medium-sized tart apples, pared, cored and coarsely chopped
1½ cups chopped mixed candied peel
3 cups raisins
3 cups golden raisins
3 cups currants
¼ cup whole blanched almonds, slivered
1½ cups dark brown sugar
¼ teaspoon ground cloves
¼ teaspoon ground nutmeg
½ teaspoon ground cinnamon
½ teaspoon ground allspice
grated rind and juice of 1 lemon
¾ cup rum, brandy or whiskey

Makes about 15 cups.

Method
Combine the suet, apples, candied peel and raisins and pass through the coarse blade of a grinder. Add the remaining ingredients and mix thoroughly.

Pack the mixture into glass jars or crocks and seal with tight-fitting lids or with several layers of plastic wrap, tied down firmly with string. Store in a dry place.

Mince Pies

2 cup quantity of rich pie pastry (made with 2 cups flour, ½ teaspoon salt, ⅔ cup butter, 2 teaspoons sugar, 1 egg yolk, 3–4 tablespoons cold water)
granulated sugar (for sprinkling)

For filling
3 cups mincemeat
1–2 tablespoons brandy, rum or sherry

3½–4 inch and 2½–3 inch cookie cutters; 2½–3 inch tartlet pans

Method
Make the pie pastry dough and chill 30 minutes. Set oven at hot (400°F).

Roll out half the dough fairly thinly and stamp out rounds with the small cutter; add the trimmings to the remaining dough and roll out thinner than before. Stamp out an equal number of rounds with the large cutter.

Mix the brandy, rum or sherry with the mincemeat. Press the larger rounds into the tartlet pans, easing out the folds. Fill them two-thirds full with mincemeat and place the smaller rounds on top.

Pinch the edges of each pie together, brush the surface lightly with cold water and sprinkle with sugar. Bake 15–20 minutes in heated oven until pastry is lightly browned and mincemeat is bubbling. Cool slightly before taking from the pans and serve hot or cold. Serve with rum or brandy hard sauce if you like.

Rum Hard Sauce

2–3 tablespoons rum (or to taste)
6 tablespoons unsalted butter
6 tablespoons dark brown sugar
grated rind of ½ lemon and squeeze of lemon juice

Method
Cream the butter and gradually beat in the sugar with the lemon rind and juice. When soft and light, beat in enough rum, a little at a time, to flavor the butter well. Pile in a small bowl and chill before serving.

Brandy Hard Sauce

Make in the same way as rum butter using 6 tablespoons unsalted butter, 6 tablespoons dark brown sugar, 2–3 tablespoons brandy (or to taste) and the same quantity of lemon rind and juice.

Cream of beet soup is garnished with chopped chives and served with croûtons (recipe is on page 92)

AN OFFBEAT DINNER

Breast of lamb, stuffed with kidneys, ham and spinach, is the tempting entrée of this dinner. For an appetizer, take your choice from a colorful beet soup, garnished with croûtons and chives or delicious deviled mushrooms, baked in whipped cream and spices. The Belvoir cake dessert is spiked with candied cherries and served with a hard sauce, or try your hand at apple soufflé.

With any lamb dish, it is hard to find a better native wine than that made chiefly from the cabernet sauvignon grape. This provides a boldness of character and touch of astringency that is particularly welcome with this meat.

A comparably authoritative imported wine would be a red from one of the better châteaux of Pomerol — hopefully, five or more years old.

Cream of Beet Soup
or
Deviled Mushrooms

Breast of Lamb Fallette

Scandinavian Potatoes   Cabbage Lorraine

Belvoir Cake with Rum or Lemon Hard Sauce
or
Apple Soufflé

Red Wine — Pomerol (Bordeaux)
or Cabernet Sauvignon (California)

TIMETABLE

Day before
Make soup and purée it, but do not add cornstarch and cream for thickening. Make the breadcrumbs for the lamb stuffing.

Morning
Prepare all the vegetables needed for the lamb. Prepare vegetables for cabbage Lorraine, cover and chill.
Cut the bread for toast to serve with the deviled mushrooms.
Make the stuffing for the lamb, stuff and sew up meat. Line casserole with bacon and add vegetables ready for braising.
Make the brown sauce for lamb.
Prepare hard sauce to serve with Belvoir cake.
Peel and slice potatoes and keep in cold water.

Assemble ingredients for final cooking from 6 p.m. for dinner around 8 p.m.

Order of Work

6:00
Set oven at moderate (350°F).

You will find that **cooking times** given in the individual recipes for these dishes have sometimes been adapted in the timetable to help you when cooking and serving this menu as a party meal.

Start cooking bacon and vegetables for lamb.

6:15
Put lamb in oven.

6:45
Prepare Belvoir cake.
Cook applesauce mixture for soufflé and beat in egg yolks.

7:00
Bake the cake *or whip egg whites for soufflé and fold into apple mixture. Transfer to dish ready for baking.*
Start to cook potatoes.

7:15
Cook and refresh cabbage, cook onion and tomatoes, add to the cabbage and put in oven.

7:30
Make the toast and sauté the mushrooms. Spoon over the devil mixture.

7:45
Take potatoes and Belvoir cake from oven and keep warm.
Remove cabbage from oven and keep hot.
Take lamb from oven, *turn up heat, put in mushrooms and bake 5–10 minutes until brown.*
Arrange the lamb on platter and keep hot.
Reheat the soup and thicken.
Add the sour cream or yogurt to the cabbage.

8:00
Serve appetizer.
Bake soufflé about 20 minutes before you are ready for dessert.

Appetizer

Cream of Beet Soup

3–4 medium beets, cooked, skinned and grated
1 medium onion, finely chopped
2 tablespoons butter
1½ tablespoons flour
3 cups chicken stock
salt and pepper
1 teaspoon red wine vinegar
½ teaspoon prepared mustard
2 teaspoons cornstarch
3 tablespoons light cream
1 tablespoon chopped chives
3–4 slices of bread, diced and fried in 3–4 tablespoons oil and butter, mixed (for croûtons) – to serve

Beets can be either boiled or baked for cream of beet soup.

Method
Cook the onion in the butter until soft but not browned. Stir in the flour, cook 1–2 minutes without browning and pour in the stock. Bring to a boil, stirring constantly, add the grated beets, season well and add the wine vinegar. Simmer the soup gently for about 20 minutes.

Work soup through a sieve or purée in a blender. Return it to the pan and stir in the mustard. Mix the cornstarch with the cream until smooth and add to the soup. Cook, stirring constantly, until the soup comes to a boil. Simmer 3 minutes and taste for seasoning.

Before serving, garnish each bowl with chives and croûtons.

Grate the cooked beets before adding to the stock mixture

Preparation of Beets

To boil beets: scrub them, taking care not to break the skin. Leave on the roots and about 1 inch of the stems. Cover the beets with cold water, add a lid and simmer 30–60 minutes, depending on the age and size of the beets.

A good test is to remove one of the beets and rub off a small piece of skin. If it comes off easily, the beets are cooked.

Cool in the cooking liquid, then trim off the roots and stems and slip off the skins with your fingers.

To bake beets: wash them, then leave on the roots and 1 inch of the stems and wrap them in foil. Place them in a baking dish and bake in a moderately low oven (325°F) for 30–60 minutes, depending on the age and size of the beets.

Remove the roots and stems and, when cool, skin the beets as above.

Alternative appetizer

Deviled Mushrooms

3 cups (¾ lb) mushrooms
2 tablespoons butter
salt and pepper
squeeze of lemon juice
4 slices of hot buttered toast
   (for serving)

For devil mixture
¾ cup heavy cream, whipped
   until it holds a soft shape
dash of Tabasco
1 tablespoon ketchup
1 teaspoon prepared
   horseradish
1 tablespoon Worcestershire
   sauce
squeeze of lemon juice
pinch of grated nutmeg
1 teaspoon Dijon-style mustard

Method
Set oven at hot (425°F).

Trim the stems and wipe the mushrooms with a damp cloth. Fry them quickly in the butter for about 1 minute. Season well, adding a squeeze of lemon juice.

Trim the crusts from the toast, place the slices in a gratin dish and arrange the mushrooms on top.

To prepare the devil mixture: beat all the ingredients into the whipped cream and continue beating until the mixture holds a peak.

Spread deviled mixture over mushrooms; bake in heated oven for 5–10 minutes or until the tops are golden.

Hot deviled mushrooms are served on slices of hot buttered toast

Breast of lamb fallette is served with brown sauce separately and cabbage Lorraine

Entrée

Breast of Lamb Fallette

2 small lean breasts of lamb
   (1½–2 lb each), boned
3–4 slices of bacon
1 large onion, diced
2 carrots, diced
2 stalks of celery, diced
bouquet garni
1½ cups well-flavored stock
2 tablespoons chopped parsley
   (for garnish)

For stuffing
2 lamb's kidneys
¾ cup finely chopped cooked
   ham
½ clove of garlic, crushed
¾ cup fresh white breadcrumbs
1 cup finely chopped fresh
   spinach leaves
1 small egg, beaten to mix
salt and pepper

For brown sauce
2 shallots, finely chopped
2 tablespoons butter
1½ tablespoons flour
1½ teaspoons tomato paste
2 cups brown stock
bouquet garni

Trussing needle and string

Method
Set oven at moderate (350°F).

Split the boned breasts of
lamb carefully at the side to
form a pocket in each one.
Spread bacon on the bottom of
a deep flameproof casserole
and put the diced vegetables
on top. Cover the casserole
and set over low heat for 5
minutes to soften the vegetables.

To prepare the stuffing:
remove the skin and cores
from the kidneys and cut them
in half. Chop them and mix
with ham and garlic. Stir in
the breadcrumbs, spinach,
egg and seasoning.

Fill the lamb pockets with
stuffing, taking care not to
stuff them too full and sew
up the openings with fine
string.

Place the lamb breasts on
the vegetables in the casserole, add bouquet garni
and pour in the well-flavored
stock. Put the lamb in heated
oven, uncovered, and cook for
1–1½ hours, basting occasionally.

To make the brown sauce:
cook the shallots in 1 tablespoon butter until they are
soft but not browned. Stir in
the remaining tablespoon
butter, blend in the flour and
cook the mixture over low
heat until it browns. Draw
the pan aside and add the
tomato paste and stock.
Bring the sauce to a boil, add
bouquet garni, season lightly
and simmer, uncovered, for
20–25 minutes, skimming if
necessary. Strain.

When the lamb is brown
and tender, remove it from
the casserole and place on a
heated platter. Remove the
string, coat with a little of the
sauce and sprinkle chopped
parsley on top.

Serve the remaining sauce
separately. Serve with cabbage Lorraine and Scandinavian potatoes.

*Sew up the stuffed breasts of
lamb with a trussing needle
and string*

Accompaniments to entrée

Scandinavian Potatoes

8 medium potatoes
¼ cup butter
salt
¼ cup grated Parmesan cheese
2 tablespoons fine
   breadcrumbs

Method
Set oven at moderate (350°F).

Peel the potatoes, wash
and pat them dry with paper
towels. With a sharp knife,
cut each potato in fairly thin
slices, almost all the way
through. The potato should
hold together and look like a
small accordion.

Melt 2 tablespoons of the
butter in a flameproof dish
large enough to hold the
potatoes. Roll the potatoes
around in the butter until
they are thoroughly coated.
Sprinkle with salt and dot
with the remaining butter.
Bake in heated oven for about
25 minutes, basting occasionally with the butter. Sprinkle
the cheese and breadcrumbs
on top and bake, without
basting, for 20–30 minutes
longer or until the potatoes
are tender when tested with
the point of a small sharp
knife.

Cabbage Lorraine

1 firm head of green cabbage
1 medium onion, finely sliced
2–3 tablespoons olive oil or
   butter
4 tomatoes, peeled, seeded
   and sliced
salt and pepper
½ cup stock (optional)
1 cup sour cream or yogurt
1 tablespoon chopped parsley

Method
Set oven at moderate (350°F).

Trim the cabbage and put
the whole head in a large pan
of boiling salted water. Simmer 4–5 minutes. Drain,
refresh and drain again,
pressing the cabbage to
remove all water. Cut the
head in quarters and remove
the hard stem. Tuck in the
tips of the leaves and pack
the quarters neatly into an
ovenproof dish or casserole.

Cook the onion in the olive
oil or butter until soft, add
the tomatoes, season with
salt and pepper and cook 5
minutes or until the tomatoes
are tender but not soft.

Spoon the tomato mixture
over the cabbage, cover the
dish or casserole with foil,
then with the lid, and bake in
heated oven for 20–30 minutes or until the cabbage is
tender. After the first 6–7
minutes, add a little of the
stock if the mixture looks dry.
This depends on the cabbage
– if it is really fresh the juice
from the tomatoes will be
enough.

When the cabbage is ten-
der, spoon the sour cream or
yogurt over the top. Return
the dish or casserole to the
oven for 4–5 minutes to
reheat thoroughly. Sprinkle
with chopped parsley before
serving.

For Belvoir cake, beat the chopped candied cherries and eggs into the creamed butter and sugar mixture

Lemon Hard Sauce

6 tablespoons butter
grated rind of 1 lemon and
    juice of $\frac{1}{2}$ lemon
$\frac{1}{4}$ cup confectioners' sugar

Makes $\frac{3}{4}$ cup.

Method
In a bowl soften the butter with the lemon rind. Add the confectioners' sugar a little at a time, with the lemon juice and beat until the mixture is light and fluffy.

Pile the hard sauce in a small bowl and chill until very firm before serving.

Dessert

Belvoir Cake

$\frac{1}{4}$ cup chopped candied red and
    green cherries
1 cup self-rising flour
pinch of salt
1 tablespoon dry instant coffee
2 tablespoons water
$\frac{1}{2}$ cup butter
$\frac{1}{2}$ cup sugar
2 eggs, lightly beaten
granulated sugar (for
    sprinkling)

Plain or fluted cake pan, ring mold or small loaf pan (3 cup capacity)

Method
Butter the pan and sprinkle it with flour, shaking out the excess. Set oven at moderate (350°F).

If the candied cherries are very sticky, rinse them quickly in hot water and pat dry with paper towels. Chop and mix them thoroughly with 1 tablespoon of the measured flour until coated. Sift the remaining flour with the salt. Dissolve the coffee in the water.

Cream the butter in a bowl and gradually beat in the sugar until the mixture is light and fluffy. Beat in the eggs, a little at a time, then fold in flour, coffee and candied cherries with a large, metal spoon.

Spoon the batter into the prepared pan and bake in heated oven for about 35—40 minutes or until a thin skewer inserted in the center comes out dry.

Remove the cake from the pan, turn out onto a warm platter and sprinkle with granulated sugar. Serve warm with a hard sauce.

To Prepare a Soufflé Dish

Rub the dish well with butter and sprinkle with sugar for a sweet soufflé, discarding excess.

Make a collar by cutting a strip of wax or silicone doubled paper 6—7 inches wide and long enough to overlap about 3 inches around dish. Make a 2 inch fold along the bottom. Butter strip above this fold and wrap the band around the outside of dish, with the folded piece at the base and turned in. This keeps paper upright.

Tie paper securely with string around dish to hold mixture as it rises.

Alternative dessert

Apple Soufflé

$1\frac{1}{2}$ cups tart applesauce,
    homemade or commercial
$\frac{1}{3}$ cup apricot jam
3 egg yolks
5 egg whites
$\frac{1}{4}$ cup sugar
confectioners' sugar (for
    sprinkling)

Soufflé dish (1 quart capacity)

Method
Prepare the soufflé dish and tie around a paper collar (see box). Set oven at hot (425°F).

Cook the applesauce and apricot jam, stirring occasionally, until the mixture is quite thick but still falls easily from the spoon. Take from the heat and beat in the egg yolks, one by one.

Beat the egg whites until they hold a stiff peak, beat in the sugar until the mixture is glossy and, using a metal spoon, fold one-quarter of the meringue into the warm apple mixture. Add the remaining meringue and fold together as lightly as possible.

Transfer the apple mixture to the prepared dish and bake at once in heated oven for 15—20 minutes or until the soufflé is puffed and brown. Remove the paper collar, sprinkle the top with confectioners' sugar and serve at once.

Sprinkle the Belvoir cake generously with granulated sugar and serve with rum or lemon hard sauce

A typical Italian dish is stufato di manzo alla romana — braised beef Roman-style — served with polenta balls (recipes are on page 103)

ITALIAN COOKING

European cuisine as we know it began not in France, but in Italy. Italian cooks of the Renaissance started with the traditions of the ancient Romans and refined their techniques. Then, when Catherine de Medici married Henri II of France in 1533, she brought skilled Italian cooks with her who introduced the new art of cooking to France.

Today Italian cooking is still excellent but largely localized and both cooking traditions and products are regional. For example, olive oil is a staple in southern Italian cooking but the dishes of northern Italy are usually made with butter.

Authentic Italian dishes demand the right ingredients. Oval, plum tomatoes have a much richer flavor than regular round tomatoes. Use Italian or Greek olives whenever possible as American olives are cured quite differently. Vegetables in many parts of Italy tend to be limited but those that are available are superb — tiny zucchini and baby eggplant; red, yellow and green peppers, and baby globe artichokes.

Italian dishes are beautiful in color — the greens of spinach and artichokes, the bright reds of tomatoes and pimientos and the delicate cream shades of pasta and veal.

In general, Italians like simple, fresh flavors that are uncomplicated by a wide variety of ingredients — freshly caught seafood cooked with olive oil and sprinkled with lemon juice; antipasti of thinly sliced smoked meats, anchovies and a few local olives; ice creams and sherbets renowned for their distinctive flavors — all these dishes are typical of modern Italian cooking.

As in most countries, in Italy no feast is complete without a traditional dessert. Usually bought at the local bakery, these are lavishly decorated, liqueur-drenched cakes that are often smothered in cream and sometimes served as a mid-morning or afternoon treat with coffee or an aperitif. But for everyday meals, dessert is more likely to consist of fresh fruit and cheese; cake, if any, may be homemade, and is simple and inexpensive. The recipes that follow are representative of dishes from all parts of Italy.

Stracciatella is a Roman specialty; serve as soon as the egg mixture starts breaking into strands

Stracciatella

1 quart well-flavored chicken stock, free from fat
3 small or 2 large eggs
½ cup grated Parmesan cheese
2 tablespoons fine semolina

This simple soup is a Roman specialty that is known throughout Italy. Semolina is obtainable at Italian and Greek grocery stores.

Method
In a pan bring the stock to a boil.

Beat the eggs with a fork until thoroughly mixed and add the cheese and semolina. Stir in ¼ cup of the hot stock, then pour this mixture into the remaining boiling stock, whisking vigorously.

Lower heat and simmer 2 minutes, beating the soup constantly — the egg mixture should be just breaking into strands. Serve at once.

Zuppa di Vongole
(Clam Soup)

3–4 dozen cherrystone clams
1 cup white wine
1 onion, finely chopped
¼ cup olive oil
1 clove of garlic, crushed
½ lb Italian-type plum tomatoes, peeled, seeded and chopped
1 tablespoon chopped parsley
1 teaspoon oregano
1 cup bottled clam juice
1 cup water
salt and pepper

For croûtons
3–4 slices of bread, crusts removed and diced
¼ cup olive oil

Method
Scrub the clams thoroughly and discard any that are open or do not shut at once when tapped.

Put the clams in a large kettle, add the wine, cover, cook over high heat, stirring once, for 7–10 minutes or until the clams open. Discard any that do not open. Strain the liquid and reserve.

To make croûtons: in a skillet or frying pan, heat the oil and fry the bread until golden brown; drain on paper towels and reserve.

In a saucepan fry the onion in the oil until golden. Add the garlic, tomatoes, parsley, oregano, clam juice and water and boil steadily for 10 minutes. Add this to the clams with the reserved liquid, bring just to a boil, taste for seasoning and serve the soup with croûtons.

Tomatoes for Pasta

Italian-type plum tomatoes give a characteristically rich flavor to Italian dishes because of their mellow taste. When fresh plum tomatoes are not available, substitute fresh regular or garden tomatoes only when they are vine-ripened and full of juice. Otherwise use canned Italian-type plum tomatoes.

Allow about 3 large regular tomatoes or 2 cups canned tomatoes to the pound. If you use regular or garden tomatoes, strengthen the color and flavor by adding 1–2 teaspoons tomato paste or ½ cup tomato purée.

Salt Cod alla Napolitana

1½ lb salt cod
2 tablespoons flour
¼ cup olive oil (for frying)

For tomato sauce
½ lb Italian-type plum tomatoes, seeded and sliced
1 tablespoon olive oil
2 cloves of garlic, sliced
salt and pepper
1 tablespoon capers
12 ripe olives, pitted
pinch of cayenne
1 slice of canned pimiento, drained and chopped

Method
Soak the cod for about 8 hours in several changes of cold water. Drain, remove the bones and any skin and divide the fish into 2 inch squares. Dry on paper towels, sprinkle lightly with flour and fry quickly in olive oil until golden brown on all sides. Drain and place in a baking dish.

To make the tomato sauce: heat the oil and fry the garlic over gentle heat for a few minutes until golden brown. Lift out and discard. Add the tomatoes with seasoning and cook 10–15 minutes or until they are soft and pulpy. Work them through a strainer or food mill and return to the pan with the capers, olives, cayenne and pimiento. Simmer 2–3 minutes and spoon this sauce over the cod.

Cover the dish with foil or a lid and bake in a moderate oven (350°F) for 15–20 minutes or until the cod flakes easily when tested with a fork.

Calamari al Pomodoro
(Squid with Tomatoes)

4–6 small squid
¼ cup olive oil
3 onions, sliced
2 tomatoes, peeled, seeded and chopped
1 tablespoon tomato paste
3 cloves of garlic, crushed
½ teaspoon oregano
½ teaspoon thyme
1 cup red wine
1 cup water
salt and pepper

Method
To clean the squid: slit open the belly and remove the bone. Immerse the squid in warm water and pull off the purplish outer skin. Remove the sac of dark ink from near the bone; rinse the squid thoroughly. Cut the tentacles into 1 inch pieces and the body into rings.

In a large skillet or shallow flameproof casserole, heat the oil and fry the onions until they are browned. Add the tomatoes, tomato paste, garlic, oregano and thyme, cover and cook gently for 5 minutes. Add the wine and simmer, uncovered, for 5 minutes. Add the water and seasoning, cover and cook gently for 1½ hours or until the squid rings are tender.

Watchpoint: do not let the squid boil or the pieces will become very tough and rubbery. Also, do not overcook them.

The mixture should be thick; if not, remove the lid towards the end of cooking so the liquid evaporates. Taste for seasoning and serve with boiled rice.

For fish alla romana, after browning fish squares cook them with peppers, tomatoes and onions

Fish alla Romana

2 lb fresh cod, haddock or
   other firm white fish
2 tablespoons flour
$\frac{1}{2}$ cup olive oil
3 green peppers, cored,
   seeded and cut in strips
2 onions, sliced
$\frac{1}{2}$ lb Italian-type plum tomatoes,
   peeled, seeded and cut in
   strips
salt and pepper
1 tablespoon chopped parsley

Method
Remove any skin and bones from the fish; wash and divide it into 2 inch squares; dry on paper towels and sprinkle with flour.

In a large skillet or flame-proof casserole heat half the olive oil and fry the fish squares quickly until golden brown on all sides. Drain well and reserve.

Blanch the peppers, drain, refresh and drain again.

Add the remaining oil to the pan and fry the onion slowly until golden. Add the tomatoes and cook gently for about 15 minutes or until thick and pulpy. Add the peppers and seasoning, then replace the fish squares, spooning the tomato mixture on top. Cover and simmer gently for 10 minutes or until the fish flakes easily when tested with a fork.

Transfer the fish mixture to a serving dish or serve in the casserole, sprinkled with parsley.

Saltimbocca

8–12 small thin veal escalopes
   ($1\frac{1}{4}$–$1\frac{1}{2}$ lb)
4–6 thin slices of cooked ham
   or prosciutto
8–12 fresh sage leaves or
   $\frac{1}{2}$ teaspoon dried sage
$\frac{1}{4}$ cup clarified butter
$\frac{1}{4}$ cup Marsala
salt and pepper

8–12 wooden toothpicks

Method
Place the veal escalopes between 2 sheets of wax paper and pound them as thinly as possible with a mallet or rolling pin.

Cut the ham or prosciutto into pieces the same size as the veal. Lay a slice of ham or prosciutto on each piece of veal and top with a leaf of fresh sage or a pinch of dried sage. Roll up neatly and secure with a toothpick.

In a skillet heat the butter and cook the veal rolls slowly until well browned on all sides. Pour over the marsala, season, cover the pan tightly and simmer 12–15 minutes or until the veal rolls are very tender.

Costolette Bolognese

4 veal cutlets
$\frac{1}{4}$ cup seasoned flour, made
   with $\frac{1}{4}$ teaspoon salt and
   pinch of pepper
1 egg, beaten with 1 tablespoon
   oil (for coating)
$\frac{1}{2}$ cup dry white breadcrumbs
   (for coating)
4 slices of cooked lean ham
$\frac{1}{4}$ cup clarified butter
3 tablespoons grated Parmesan
   cheese
2 tablespoons butter (for
   sprinkling)

Method
Trim the cutlets, place them between 2 sheets of wax paper and pound with a mallet or rolling pin until the meat is $\frac{1}{4}$ inch thick; snip the edges so they do not curl.

Coat them thoroughly with seasoned flour, brush with beaten egg and oil mixture and coat with breadcrumbs, pressing them in well with a metal spatula.

Trim the slices of ham the same size and shape as the veal.

In a skillet heat the clarified butter and fry the cutlets gently for 5 minutes on each side or until golden brown. Place a slice of ham over each piece of veal and sprinkle with cheese. Melt the 2 table-spoons butter carefully so it does not get too hot and sprinkle over the cheese.

Cover the pan and cook very gently for 3–4 minutes longer or until the cheese melts. Serve with a vegetable like zucchini or fennel in béchamel sauce.

Fennel in Béchamel Sauce

2 large bulbs of fennel
béchamel sauce, made with
   2 tablespoons butter,
   2 tablespoons flour, $1\frac{1}{2}$ cups
   milk (infused with slice of
   onion, 6 peppercorns, blade
   of mace and bay leaf)
2 tablespoons heavy cream
salt and pepper
2 tablespoons browned
   breadcrumbs
2 tablespoons melted butter

Method

Wash the fennel bulbs, trim the stalks and roots and cut each bulb into 8 pieces. Cook in boiling salted water for 6—8 minutes or until tender. Drain.

Meanwhile make the béchamel sauce, stir in the cream and season well.

Arrange the fennel in an ovenproof dish, spoon over the sauce to coat and sprinkle with browned breadcrumbs. Dot with melted butter and bake in a hot oven (400°F) for 7—10 minutes or until bubbling and browned.

Fennel is a bulbous white root that looks a little like a fat celery heart. It is related to herb fennel and has a pleasant flavor of anise. Fennel can be sliced and used raw in salads or it can be cooked.

Stufato di Manzo alla Romana

(Braised Beef Roman-style)

$2-2\frac{1}{2}$ lb beef round or rump
1 tablespoon oil
2 tablespoons butter
2 onions, chopped
2 cloves of garlic, crushed
$\frac{1}{4}$ lb salt pork, diced and
   blanched
1 tablespoon flour
$\frac{1}{2}$ cup red wine
$1\frac{1}{2}-2$ cups beef stock
bouquet garni
1 lb Italian-type plum tomatoes,
   peeled, seeded and cut in 8
salt and pepper
polenta balls (for serving)

Method

Set oven at moderate (350°F).

In a large flameproof casserole heat the oil and butter and brown the beef on all sides. Take it out and add the onion, garlic and pork and fry 5 minutes or until just beginning to brown. Stir in the flour and cook until lightly browned, then pour on the wine and $1\frac{1}{2}$ cups stock. Add bouquet garni, season and bring the mixture to a boil.

Replace the beef, cover the casserole and braise in heated oven for $2-2\frac{1}{2}$ hours or until the beef is tender, adding more stock if the liquid reduces rapidly. Add the tomatoes to the casserole 30 minutes before the end of cooking.

Take out the beef, carve in $\frac{1}{4}$ inch slices and arrange in a serving dish. Skim the sauce and discard bouquet garni; boil to reduce the sauce slightly and taste for seasoning.

Spoon the sauce over and around the beef and pile polenta balls at each end of the dish.

Polenta Balls

$\frac{1}{2}$ cup yellow cornmeal
2 cups water
1 tablespoon butter
1 egg
1 tablespoon grated Parmesan
   cheese
salt and pepper
$\frac{1}{2}$ teaspoon Dijon-style mustard
   (or to taste)

For coating
1 egg, beaten to mix
$\frac{1}{2}$ cup dry white breadcrumbs
deep fat (for frying)

Fat thermometer (optional)

Makes 12 balls.

Method

Bring the water to a boil, stir in the cornmeal and cook over low heat, stirring often, for 12—15 minutes or until the mixture is very thick. Take from heat and beat in the butter, egg and cheese; season well with salt, pepper and mustard. Spread the mixture on a plate to cool.

Divide the mixture and roll on a floured board into $1\frac{1}{2}$ inch balls. Brush them with beaten egg and coat with dry breadcrumbs. Fry polenta balls in hot deep fat (375°F on a fat thermometer) until golden brown and drain thoroughly on paper towels.

Serve with stufato di manzo alla romana.

Involtini alla Milanese

1 pork tenderloin (about 1 lb),
   or 1 lb veal escalopes
$\frac{1}{2}$ cup ($\frac{1}{4}$ lb) ground fresh pork
1 cup ($\frac{1}{2}$ lb) loose pork sausage
   meat
1 clove of garlic, crushed
1 tablespoon chopped parsley
$1\frac{1}{2}$ tablespoons grated
   Parmesan cheese
pinch of ground nutmeg
salt
black pepper, freshly ground
1 egg, beaten to mix
10—12 slices of bacon
2 tablespoons flour
2 tablespoons butter
$\frac{3}{4}$ cup white wine

Wooden toothpicks

Method

Cut the pork tenderloin into thin slices or divide the escalopes into 2—3 pieces. Place the pieces of pork or veal between 2 sheets of wax paper and pound with a mallet or rolling pin until very thin.

Combine the ground pork, sausage meat, garlic, parsley, cheese and nutmeg and season lightly; add enough beaten egg to bind the mixture. Spread a layer of this stuffing on each slice of pork or veal and roll them up. Wrap each roll in a slice of bacon and fasten with a toothpick; sprinkle with flour.

Set oven at moderate (350°F).

In a skillet or shallow flameproof casserole heat the butter, add the meat rolls and fry gently until golden brown all over. Pour over the wine and simmer until reduced by half.

Cover the pan tightly and bake in heated oven for 30—40 minutes or until the meat rolls are tender. Serve with risotto milanese (see page 104).

Risotto Milanese

1¼ cups round grain rice
1 marrow bone (optional)
¼ cup butter
1 small onion, finely chopped
1 clove of garlic, chopped or crushed
pinch of saffron, soaked in 2 tablespoons hot water for 30 minutes (optional)
about 3 cups chicken or veal stock
salt and pepper
2–3 tablespoons grated Parmesan cheese

Sliced mushrooms (about ½ cup) are sometimes added to this risotto with the onion. For special occasions, use ½ cup white wine in place of the same amount of stock.

Method
Scoop the marrow from the bone and cut into small pieces. Melt half the butter in a shallow pan or flameproof casserole, add the marrow, onion and garlic and fry gently for 4–5 minutes. Add the rice and continue to fry 4–5 minutes, stirring continuously until all the grains look white.

Add the saffron liquid and about a third of the stock. Season and simmer uncovered, stirring occasionally, until the rice thickens, then add another third of stock. Continue cooking until the rice thickens again. Add the remaining stock and cook until the grains are barely tender and the risotto is creamy.

Take the pan from heat, dot the surface of the risotto with the remaining butter and sprinkle with the Parmesan cheese. Cover the rice and leave 5 minutes or until ready to serve. Stir once or twice with a fork, then turn into a hot serving dish. Avoid using a spoon as this makes the rice mushy.

Note: bone marrow is very characteristic of a risotto milanese, but both it and the saffron may be omitted. If more convenient, the marrow bone may be boiled before scooping out the marrow, and this should be added to the risotto towards the end of cooking. In either case, use the bone to make stock.

Spezzatino di Pollo alla Trasteverina
(Baked Chicken with Mushrooms, Peppers and Zucchini)

2 (1½–2 lb each) frying chickens
½ cup seasoned flour, made with ½ teaspoon salt and ¼ teaspoon pepper
½ cup olive oil
¼ lb salt pork, diced
2 cloves of garlic, crushed
½ cup white wine
1 cup (¼ lb) small mushrooms
2 yellow or red peppers, cored, seeded and cut in strips
4 small zucchini, sliced
½ lb Italian-type plum tomatoes, peeled, seeded and chopped
½ teaspoon rosemary
1 teaspoon marjoram
1 tablespoon chopped parsley
salt and pepper

Method
Cut each chicken in 4 pieces discarding the backbone. Coat them thoroughly in seasoned flour.

In a skillet or flameproof casserole, heat the oil and fry the chicken pieces, a few at a time, over medium heat until brown on all sides. Put the chicken legs back in the pan, cover and cook over gentle heat for 10 minutes. Add the breasts, cover and cook 15 minutes longer or until very tender. Take from pan and keep warm.

Blanch the pork for 10 minutes and drain, add to the fat in the pan and fry until golden brown. Take out and reserve.

Drain off all but 2 tablespoons fat, add the garlic, cook 10 seconds, add the wine and simmer until only 2–3 tablespoons are left.

Trim the mushroom stems level with the caps and add to the pan with the peppers, zucchini, tomatoes and herbs. Season, cover and cook gently for 10 minutes or until the zucchini and mushrooms are tender. Add the salt pork and chicken pieces, mix lightly and cook 5 minutes longer.

Arrange the chicken pieces on a hot platter, spoon the vegetables and juice on top and serve.

Insalati di Legumi
(Vegetable Salad)

1 large red or Bermuda onion, sliced and separated into rings
2 cucumbers, peeled and sliced
10–12 radishes
2 small celery hearts, sliced
salsa verde (for serving)

Method
Blanch the onion in boiling water for 1 minute and drain. Put into cold water, bring again to a boil and cook 1–2 minutes; drain and refresh. The onion should be slightly crisp and not too soft.

Soak the cucumber slices in ice water for 15 minutes, then drain and dry well on paper towels.

Cut radishes in roses and soak in ice water for 30 minutes so they open, or slice them.

Arrange the cucumber, onion and celery in layers in a bowl, piling them in a pyramid. Spoon over salsa verde and garnish with radish roses or slices.

Radish Roses

Trim the tails and all but the smallest green leaves from red radishes. With a sharp knife, make several angled cuts (like tiny petals) down the radish, starting at the root end and working down to the stem end, but do not slice completely through.

Keep the radishes in a bowl of ice water so the petals will open out.

Salsa Verde
(Green Sauce)

1 cup parsley sprigs, chopped
1½ tablespoons capers
1–2 cloves of garlic, crushed
1–2 anchovy fillets, chopped
4–5 tablespoons olive oil
1 slice of white bread, crusts removed
1 tablespoon lemon juice
salt and pepper

Method
In a mortar and pestle pound the parsley with the capers, garlic and anchovies. Spoon 1–2 tablespoons oil over the bread and, when soaked, add to the parsley mixture and continue pounding until it is smooth.

Gradually work in the

Serve osso buco (baked veal shanks) with a gremolata garnish of garlic, parsley and lemon rind

remaining oil, add the lemon juice and season well — the sauce should be thick.

If you like, the sauce can also be made in the blender by combining all ingredients and blending until smooth.

Osso Buco

4 lb veal shank, cut in 2 inch
    rounds
$\frac{1}{4}$ cup butter
1 onion, sliced
1 carrot, sliced
1 cup white wine
1 lb Italian-type plum tomatoes,
    peeled, seeded and chopped
1–1$\frac{1}{2}$ cups stock
1 clove of garlic, crushed
bouquet garni
salt and pepper

For garnish
1 clove of garlic, finely chopped
$\frac{1}{4}$ cup chopped parsley
grated rind of 1 lemon

The garnish, called gremolata, is an essential part of osso buco. The dish is invariably served with risotto milanese or with plain buttered pasta.

Method
In a large skillet or shallow flameproof casserole heat the butter and, when foaming, brown the veal on both sides, 2–3 rounds at a time. Remove them, add onion and carrot, cover the pan and cook over steady heat, without stirring, for 2–3 minutes.

Replace the veal rounds with the bones upright in the pan, so the marrow cannot fall out during cooking. Add the wine and simmer until reduced by half. Add the tomatoes and cook 10 minutes longer. Add 1 cup stock, garlic, bouquet garni and seasoning, cover and bake in a moderate oven (350°F) or simmer very gently on top of

the stove for 1$\frac{1}{4}$–1$\frac{1}{2}$ hours or until the veal is so tender it almost falls from the bones. Add more stock during cooking if the pan seems dry.

Transfer the veal rounds to a serving dish and keep warm. Strain the sauce, pressing well.

Watchpoint: all the tomato pulp should go through the strainer with as little as possible of the carrots and onions.

Boil the sauce until it is well reduced and glossy.

To make the garnish: mix the garlic with the parsley and lemon rind.

Taste the sauce for seasoning, spoon it over the veal, sprinkle with the garnish and serve with risotto milanese.

Brown veal shanks well on both sides

Bone marrow gives a delicious richness to osso buco. Bone marrow can also be removed from large split bones, then cut into $\frac{1}{2}$ inch slices and fried (see recipe for risotto milanese) or poached in a little stock for about 1$\frac{1}{2}$– 2 minutes and added to a dish towards the end of cooking. Bone marrow should never be over-cooked.

All independent butchers sell marrow bones.

This version of fritto misto from Milan includes sweetbreads, brains, liver and globe artichokes

Fritto Misto alla Milanese

2 large veal escalopes
2 thin slices of calves' liver
1 pair small veal sweetbreads, prepared (see box)
1 set calf's or sheep's brains, prepared (see box)
1½–2 cups stock
1 veal or 2 lamb's kidneys
1 small cauliflower
2 medium zucchini
2 baby globe artichokes
potato croquettes (for serving)
¾ cup butter (for frying)

For coating
1 cup seasoned flour, made with 1 teaspoon salt and ½ teaspoon pepper
2 eggs, beaten to mix
2 cups dry white breadcrumbs

For sauce
¼ cup butter
juice of ½ lemon

Choose as many of the above ingredients as you like. Serves 6.

Method
Place the veal escalopes between 2 sheets of wax paper and pound them as thinly as possible with a mallet or rolling pin. Cut each into 3 pieces and coat with seasoned flour.

Coat the liver thoroughly with seasoned flour. Cut the prepared sweetbreads in ¾ inch slices, coat with seasoned flour, brush with beaten egg and coat with breadcrumbs.

Simmer the prepared brains in stock barely to cover for 15 minutes or until they are just firm. Drain the brains thoroughly on paper towels, cut in half and coat with seasoned flour. Brush with beaten egg and coat with breadcrumbs.

Skin the kidneys, cut away the cores with scissors. Slice the veal kidney or cut the lamb's kidneys in half.

Wash the cauliflower, break into flowerets and cook in boiling salted water for 8–10 minutes or until just tender. Drain thoroughly, coat with seasoned flour and dip in beaten egg.

Wash zucchini, cut in ¾ inch diagonal slices and blanch in boiling salted water for 3 minutes. Drain, refresh and drain again on paper towels, then coat with seasoned flour and dip in beaten egg.

Wash the artichokes, trim the leaves and stems and cook in boiling salted water for 20–25 minutes or until tender. Drain and cut into quarters. Baby globe artichokes do not have 'chokes' to remove.

Prepare the potato croquettes and keep hot.

In a large skillet, heat some of the butter and start frying the ingredients in the order in which they were prepared, adding more butter when necessary. When each ingredient is cooked, drain it, arrange on a large platter and keep warm.

Fry the escalopes for 3 minutes on each side over medium heat until golden brown. Fry the liver over medium heat for 2–3 minutes on each side until brown on the outside and pink in the center.

Fry the sweetbreads over brisk heat for 1–2 minutes on each side until golden brown. Fry the brains over brisk heat for 1–2 minutes on each side until golden brown. Fry the kidneys over medium heat for 2–3 minutes on each side until lightly browned and pink in the center.

Fry the cauliflower over brisk heat for 1–2 minutes until golden brown. Fry zucchini over brisk heat for 1–2 minutes on each side until golden brown. Fry the artichokes over medium heat for 2–3 minutes until golden brown. Add the cooked potato croquettes to the platter.

When all the ingredients are cooked, wipe out the skillet, add the ¼ cup butter and cook until nut brown in color. At once add the lemon juice and pour the sauce, while still foaming, over the fritto misto. Serve at once.

Potato Croquettes

Cook 3 medium potatoes in boiling salted water for 15 minutes or until tender. Drain and work through a strainer or ricer. Return to a pan and beat in 1 tablespoon butter, 1 egg yolk, 2 tablespoons hot milk, and salt and pepper.

Cool the mixture and roll on a floured board into a 1-inch thick cylinder. Cut into 2 inch lengths.

Roll the croquettes in flour, seasoned with salt and pepper, and brush with 1 egg, beaten to mix with ½ teaspoon salt. Coat with dry white breadcrumbs and fry in butter, turning so the croquettes brown evenly, or fry in deep fat (375°F on a fat thermometer). Drain well on paper towels.

To prepare brains: soak them in cold salted water for 2–3 hours. Wash them well to remove any traces of blood. Drain, blanch and drain again. Rinse and trim away skin or membrane.

Fritto misto (literally 'mixed fry') is one of those dishes that vary enormously from place to place. Ingredients can include meat, variety meats, fish, poultry and vegetables and they may be shallow fried in oil or butter or deep fried in oil. Flour, egg and breadcrumbs or fritter batter may be used as coatings.

Fritto misto alla fiorentina, for example, is very much like the **fritto misto alla milanese** given here but fewer ingredients are used and these may vary. All are coated in egg and breadcrumbs and fried in deep oil.

A typical fritto misto alla fiorentina includes sweetbreads, brains, baby lamb rib chops, tiny potato croquettes, sliced zucchini and baby artichokes.

To prepare sweetbreads: soak them in cold salted water for 3–5 hours with 1–2 slices of lemon or a few drops of vinegar. Rinse them, put in a pan and cover with water. Add a pinch of salt and another slice of lemon; bring to a boil over low heat, skimming the top occasionally. Simmer 5 minutes. Drain and rinse them quickly in cold water.

Remove any ducts and pull off the skin. Press the sweetbreads between 2 flat plates, with a 2 lb weight on top, until cold.

Red peppers make a colorful addition to many Italian dishes

Carciofi alla Barigoule
(Artichokes with Mushrooms)

4 large globe artichokes
½ cup white wine
1½ cups veal or vegetable stock
kneaded butter, made with
   1 tablespoon butter and
   ½ tablespoon flour

For filling
3 cups (¾ lb) mushrooms
3 tablespoons butter
1 medium onion, finely
   chopped
1 medium carrot, finely
   chopped
½ cup (¼ lb) ham, finely
   chopped (optional)
2 tablespoons chopped parsley
2 teaspoons mixed herbs
   (thyme, oregano, marjoram)
½ cup fresh white breadcrumbs
salt and pepper

Barigoule is the name for a type of mushroom that is popular in Italy and southern France.

Method
Trim the stalks of the artichokes and trim the leaves and tops with scissors to remove the spines. Wash them thoroughly, then cook in boiling salted water for 35–45 minutes or until they are almost tender and a leaf can be pulled away with a sharp tug. Drain, refresh and cool.

To make the filling: chop the mushrooms, reserving 4 large ones. Melt 1 tablespoon of the butter in a frying pan, add the onion and carrot and cook until soft. Add the chopped mushrooms and cook over medium heat for about 5 minutes or until all the moisture has evaporated.

Take the pan from the heat and add the ham, if used, parsley, herbs and enough breadcrumbs to make a firm but moist mixture. Season to taste.

Set oven at moderate (350°F).

Pull out the center leaves of the artichokes and scoop out the hairy chokes with a teaspoon. Fill the cavities with the mushroom mixture and top each one with a whole mushroom and a small piece of the remaining butter. Tie string around the artichokes to hold the leaves together and arrange them in a deep baking dish.

Pour around the wine and stock, cover the artichokes with foil or a lid and bake in heated oven for 35–40 minutes or until very tender. Transfer the artichokes to a platter and keep warm.

Strain the cooking liquid — there should be about 1 cup — reheat it and whisk in the kneaded butter to thicken the liquid. Simmer 2 minutes, season to taste, pour the sauce around the artichokes and serve.

Bigne di Cavolfiore
(Cauliflower Fritters)

1 large cauliflower
1 bay leaf
béchamel sauce, made with ¼
   cup butter, ¼ cup flour, 2
   cups milk (infused with slice
   of onion, 6 peppercorns,
   blade of mace and bay leaf)
deep fat (for frying)
bunch of parsley (for garnish)
1 cup tomato sauce (for
   serving)

For fritter batter
1 cup flour
½ teaspoon salt
¾ cup warm water
1 tablespoon olive oil or
   2 tablespoons melted
   butter
1 egg yolk
1 tablespoon heavy cream
   (optional)
2 egg whites

Fat thermometer (optional)

Method
Break the cauliflower into flowerets, including the stalk. Cook with the bay leaf in lightly salted water for 8–10 minutes or until barely tender. Drain and cool.

Make the béchamel sauce and cool to room temperature.

Dip the cauliflower flowerets into the cool sauce, making sure they are completely coated. Lift out, lay on a plate and chill until very firm.

To make the fritter batter: sift the flour with the salt into a bowl and make a well in the center. Add the water, oil or butter, egg yolk and cream, if used, and stir until smooth. Let stand 30 minutes.

Just before frying, beat the egg whites for the fritter batter until they hold a stiff peak and fold into the batter.

Heat deep fat to very hot (375°F on a fat thermometer), dip the cauliflower flowerets into the batter and lower them carefully into the deep fat. Fry a few flowerets at a time until they are a deep golden brown and drain on paper towels. Cool the fat slightly and fry the parsley for a few seconds until it stops sputtering. Lift out and drain.

Arrange the cauliflower fritters on a white napkin on a hot dish and garnish with sprigs of fried parsley. Serve tomato sauce separately.

Cannoli
(Cream 'Pipes')

1½ cups flour
pinch of salt
2 tablespoons sugar
about 6 tablespoons Marsala or
 sherry
deep fat (for frying)

For filling
2 cups (1 lb) ricotta cheese
½ cup sugar
¼ cup mixed chopped candied
 fruit
¼ cup shelled pistachios,
 chopped
2 squares (2 oz) semisweet
 chocolate, chopped
1 teaspoon vanilla

To finish
¼ cup chopped pistachios or
 browned, chopped almonds
confectioners' sugar
 (for sprinkling)

*8–10 cannoli tubes; pastry
bag and ½ inch plain tube*

Cannoli, meaning 'pipes', are shaped around special 1 inch metal tubes. A good substitute can be made with a double thickness of heavy duty foil, or metal cornet molds may be used. If you prefer, the ricotta cheese can be flavored with sugar and ¼ cup Marsala instead of the candied fruits, pistachios, chocolate and vanilla. Makes 8–10 cannoli.

Method
To make the pastry dough: sift the flour with the salt into a bowl, add the sugar, make a well in the center, add the Marsala or sherry and work to a smooth, fairly stiff dough, adding more wine, if necessary. Knead the dough on a lightly floured board for 10 minutes or until very smooth and elastic; cover and chill for 2 hours.

Let the dough come to room temperature, then roll as thinly as possible on a floured board and cut in 5 inch squares. Wrap each square diagonally around a tube so a corner is at each end; moisten the central overlapping corner with water and press down firmly to seal the 'pipe', leaving both ends open.

Heat the deep fat to 375°F on a fat thermometer and lower in 3–4 cannoli at a time in a frying basket. Fry them until golden brown, lift out and drain on paper towels. Continue frying the remaining cannoli. When cool, slip them off the tubes.

To make the filling: work the cheese through a sieve, then beat it with the sugar until smooth and light. Beat in the candied fruit, pistachios, chopped chocolate and vanilla.

Put the filling into the pastry bag fitted with the plain tube and pipe the mixture into the cannoli shells to fill them. Dip each end into the chopped pistachios or almonds and sprinkle the pastry with confectioners' sugar.

Zuppa Inglese

4 squares (4 oz) semisweet
 chocolate, grated
1 cup heavy cream, whipped
 until it holds a soft shape
1 package of ladyfingers
1 cup sweet white wine
¼ cup whole blanched almonds,
 chopped
2 tablespoons mixed candied
 fruit, finely chopped
 (optional)

*Glass bowl (1–1½ quart
capacity)*

Method
Melt the chocolate on a heat-proof plate over a pan of hot water and cool. When cool but not set, fold the chocolate into the whipped cream. Put the ladyfingers on a plate and sprinkle with wine.

Spread a layer of chocolate cream in the bottom of the bowl and cover with a layer of soaked ladyfingers; sprinkle with a few chopped almonds and candied fruit and continue adding layers until all the ingredients are used, ending with cream. Cover and chill 3–4 hours until the mixture is firm.

Serve the zuppa inglese plain or with cold zabaione (sabayon) sauce.

Cold
Sabayon Sauce

¼ cup sugar
¼ cup water
2 egg yolks
grated rind and juice of
 ½ lemon
1 tablespoon rum or brandy,
 or 2 tablespoons sherry
¾ cup heavy cream, whipped
 until it holds a soft shape

Makes about 1–1½ cups.

Method
Dissolve the sugar in the water over gentle heat, then boil the syrup until it spins a thread between your finger and thumb when a little is lifted on a spoon (230°F–234°F on a sugar thermometer).

Beat the egg yolks well, take the syrup from the heat and as soon as the bubbles have subsided, pour it gradually onto the egg yolks, beating constantly. Continue beating until the mixture is very thick.

Beat in the lemon rind and juice. Flavor with rum, brandy or sherry and continue to beat 1–2 minutes or until cool. Fold the whipped cream into the mixture and chill.

Zuppa inglese: the origin of this famous Italian dish probably goes back to the 19th century when British tourists started visiting Italy in large numbers. They demanded the English dessert, trifle, which is made of cake soaked in wine, jam or fruit, egg custard and whipped cream. This reminded Italian cooks of their soups – zuppas – which are often thickened with bread, so they called the dessert zuppa inglese.

There are innumerable versions, some flavored with chocolate, others with liqueur or Marsala; some are molded and others are served, layered, in a glass bowl.

Cannoli or cream 'pipes' are deep fried before filling with a ricotta cheese and candied fruit mixture

Cassata Siciliana

3 egg quantity sponge cake 1,
    baked in an 8 inch cake pan
    (see Volume 6)
3 cups (1½ lb) ricotta cheese or
    creamed cottage cheese
1½ cups sugar
9 tablespoons water
1½ teaspoons vanilla
1 teaspoon cinnamon
3 tablespoons Maraschino
    liqueur
3 squares (3 oz) semisweet
    chocolate, coarsely chopped
1½ tablespoons shelled
    pistachios, halved
¾ cup finely chopped mixed
    candied peel

For decoration
confectioners' sugar
few candied cherries
pieces of candied orange,
    lemon and citron peel

8 inch springform pan

Serves 6–8 people.

Method
Beat the ricotta or cottage
cheese in a bowl until it is as
smooth as possible.

In a small pan heat the
sugar with the water until
dissolved, then boil until it
starts to caramelize and is
just golden in color. At once
beat into the softened cheese
— at first the syrup will crystallize but later it will melt. Add
the vanilla, cinnamon, Maraschino liqueur and chocolate
and beat until smooth. Stir in
the pistachios and candied
peel.

Cut the sponge cake into 3
layers and set 1 layer in the
springform pan. Spread with
half the cheese mixture, top
with a layer of cake, add
remaining cheese mixture and
cover with the remaining layer
of cake. Cover the pan and
chill cassata several hours or

overnight — the flavor will
mellow on standing.

To serve, remove the
springform pan and sprinkle
the cassata thickly with confectioners' sugar. Decorate
the top with halved candied
cherries and thin slices of candied orange, lemon and citron
peel.

Zeppole alla Napoletana
(Fried Puffs)

1½ cups flour
1½ tablespoons semolina or
    cream of wheat
1½ cups water
6 tablespoons sugar
2 tablespoons olive oil
¼ teaspoon salt
1 bay leaf
3 egg yolks
2 tablespoons sweet Marsala
2–3 tablespoons olive oil
    (for greasing)
deep fat (for frying)
confectioners' sugar (for
    sprinkling)

Fat thermometer (optional)

Method
In a heavy saucepan heat the
water, sugar, oil, salt and bay
leaf until the sugar dissolves,
then bring to a boil.

Mix the flour with the semolina or cream of wheat, and as
soon as the sugar mixture
boils, stir in the flour mixture all
at once and take pan from heat.
Beat until the mixture is
smooth and pulls away from
the sides of the pan. Cook
over a low heat, stirring, for 5
minutes to dry the mixture.

Take from heat, discard the
bay leaf and cool the dough
slightly. Beat in the egg yolks,
one at a time, beating well
after each addition. Add the
Marsala and beat 5 minutes or
until the dough is very glossy.

Grease a marble slab or
Formica-type surface with
olive oil and spread the dough
in a rectangle on it to cool
thoroughly. Brush the top
with olive oil, fold the dough
in three (as for flaky pastry),
pat it out again, and repeat
the oiling and folding 5 times.
Then roll the dough with the
hands to a rope about three-
eighths inch thick and cut
into 6 inch lengths. Knot the
lengths loosely.

Heat the fat to 350°F on a
fat thermometer and lower
the knots into it, a few at a
time. Raise the heat slowly to
375°F so the knots cook in a
rising temperature, and fry
them until golden brown,
turning them occasionally.
Prick them with a sharp fork
during cooking so the un-
cooked dough inside can
emerge through the holes.

Drain the knots on paper
towels, sprinkle with confectioners' sugar and serve at
once.

A recipe for the famous Italian
dessert **zabaione,** also known
as **zabaglione,** will be given
in Volume 10.

Torta di Formaggio
(Cheesecake)

For pastry dough
2 cups flour
½ teaspoon salt
¾ cup butter, softened
4 egg yolks
¼ cup sugar
3 tablespoons Marsala

For filling
2 lb (4 cups) ricotta cheese
½ cup raisins
½ cup golden raisins
½ cup sugar
1 tablespoon flour
½ teaspoon salt
1 teaspoon vanilla
4 egg yolks
1 egg, beaten to mix with
    ½ teaspoon salt (for glaze)

8 inch square cake pan

Method
To make the pastry dough: sift
the flour and salt onto a board
or marble slab. Make a large
well in the center, add the
butter, egg yolks, sugar and
Marsala and work with the
fingertips of one hand until
the central ingredients are
combined.

Working with the whole
hand, gradually draw in the
flour, using the fingers and
heel of the hand in a rocking
motion. Knead the dough
lightly with the heel of the
hand until smooth and chill
30 minutes. Set oven at
moderately hot (375°F).

Roll out the pastry dough
and line the cake pan; trim
the edges and reserve the
trimmings. Bake the pastry
shell blind in heated oven
for 15 minutes and let cool
slightly. Lower oven heat
to moderate (350°F).

To make the filling: pour
boiling water over both kinds
of raisins, let stand 10–15

minutes until they are plump, drain and dry them on paper towels. Beat the cheese until it is soft and beat in the sugar, flour, salt, vanilla and egg yolks. Stir in the dry raisins.

Add the filling to the pastry shell and smooth the top. Roll out the remaining dough, cut it into thin strips and arrange them, parallel, across the top of the cheese mixture; press the ends to seal to the edges of the pastry. Brush with egg glaze and bake in heated oven for 1 hour or until the cake is browned and firm. Let cool in the pan and cut the cheesecake in bars to serve.

Italian cheesecake is cut into bars for serving

Tagliatelle al prosciutto, tossed with butter and Parmesan cheese, has a ham and tomato sauce spooned over (recipe is on page 116)

HOW TO COOK PASTA (2)

We think of pasta as typically Italian but it is only in the last 150 years, since mechanical pasta cutters were invented, that it has become an indispensable part of almost any Italian meal. Despite the convenience of commercial products, home-made pasta is still the pride of accomplished Italian cooks and, in this lesson, we give recipes for fresh canneloni, fettucine, lasagne and tagliatelle; a recipe for fresh ravioli was given in Volume 5. Commercial pasta can be used instead of fresh pasta in all these recipes, and it will take 2–5 minutes longer to cook, depending on the kind used.

Tagliatelle and Fettucine Dough

3 cups flour
½ teaspoon salt
2 eggs
5 tablespoons milk

Method

Sift the flour with the salt onto a board or marble slab. Make a well in the center and add the eggs and milk. Start to draw the flour into the center, working the eggs and flour together with the fingers of one hand. Depending on the size of eggs, a little extra milk or extra flour may be needed to make a dough which is soft but not sticky.

Knead the dough thoroughly for 5 minutes or until very smooth and elastic. Cover and let stand 1 hour to lose some of its elasticity.

If rolling by hand, divide the dough into 2—3 pieces, roll each piece as thinly as possible and lay these on a paper over a chair back for 2 hours or longer to dry a little, then roll up each piece loosely and cut into ½—¾ inch slices (for tagliatelle) or ¼—⅜ inch slices (for fettucine). Unroll the strips, put them on a cloth or paper and dry 30 minutes longer.

If using a pasta cutting machine, divide the dough into 3—4 pieces, flatten each piece slightly and work through the machine according to the manufacturers' directions. Dry the dough for 2—3 hours before cooking.

For flavored pasta: add ¼ cup cooked puréed spinach or 2 tablespoons tomato paste to the eggs before mixing the dough, and add only 3 tablespoons milk.

Tagliatelle al Prosciutto

3 cup quantity of fresh tagliatelle dough
½ lb uncooked country ham, diced
6 tablespoons butter
1 carrot, chopped
3—4 stalks of celery, chopped
1—2 cloves of garlic, crushed
1½ tablespoons tomato paste
¾ cup well-flavored veal or beef stock
black pepper, freshly ground
salt
¼ cup grated Parmesan cheese

Method

Melt 4 tablespoons butter in a skillet, add the ham and fry gently for 5 minutes or until lightly browned. Add the carrot, celery and garlic, cover and cook 4—5 minutes. Stir in the tomato paste and stock with pepper and salt, if needed, and simmer, uncovered for 5 minutes or until the mixture is slightly thickened. Keep warm.

Cook the tagliatelle in plenty of boiling salted water for 8—10 minutes or until it is tender but still firm ('al dente'). Stir occasionally to prevent it from sticking. Drain it, rinse with hot water and return to the pan with remaining butter and seasoning and toss over heat until very hot.

Add the cheese, pile into a serving dish and spoon over the ham and tomato sauce.

Tortelli

3 cup quantity of fresh tagliatelle dough
1 cup (½ lb) ricotta or creamed cottage cheese
½ cup grated Parmesan cheese
1 egg
1 egg yolk
salt and pepper
pinch of ground allspice
1 tablespoon chopped parsley
3 tablespoons melted butter (for serving)

2½ inch cookie cutter

Method

Mix the ricotta or cottage cheese with the Parmesan cheese, reserving 2 tablespoons Parmesan, and beat until smooth. Beat in the egg, egg yolk, seasoning, allspice and parsley.

Roll out the dough very thinly. Cut out circles with the cookie cutter and put a teaspoon of cheese mixture in the center of each circle. Brush the edges with water, fold over like a turnover and press the edges firmly together. Let stand 30 minutes.

Drop the turnovers into a large pan of boiling salted water and simmer 15—20 minutes or until tender but still firm ('al dente'). Stir occasionally to prevent them from sticking.

Lift the tortelli out with a slotted spoon, drain well on paper towels and pile in a hot serving dish. Spoon over melted butter, sprinkle with remaining Parmesan cheese and serve very hot.

Tagliatelle Verde al Pomodoro

3 cup quantity of fresh tagliatelle dough, flavored with spinach
1 lb Italian-style plum tomatoes, peeled, seeded and cut in chunks, or 2 cups canned plum tomatoes, drained and cut in chunks
¼ cup butter
1 onion, finely chopped
grated rind of 2 lemons
salt and pepper
grated Parmesan cheese (for serving)

Method

In a skillet melt half the butter and fry the onion until it is soft but not browned. Add the tomatoes, lemon rind and seasoning and cook quickly for 1—2 minutes or until the tomatoes are just cooked, but not soft.

Cook the tagliatelle in plenty of boiling salted water for 8—10 minutes or until it is tender but still firm ('al dente'); stir it occasionally to prevent it from sticking.

Drain the pasta, rinse it with hot water and return it to the pan with the remaining butter and seasoning and toss it over heat until it is very hot. Pile the tagliatelle in a serving dish, spoon over the tomato mixture and serve grated Parmesan cheese separately.

Quantities

In this lesson, terms like '3 cup quantity' refer to the amount of dough obtained by using 3 cups flour, not 3 cups prepared dough. The **tagliatelle** and **fettucine** recipes serve 4 as an entrée and 6—8 as an appetizer.

Tagliatelle verde (green ribbon noodles) is served with tomato sauce

Fettucine alla Romagnola

3 cup quantity of fresh
   fettucine dough
   (see page 116)
1 medium onion, thinly sliced
4–5 tablespoons olive oil
2 cloves of garlic, crushed
1 lb Italian-type plum
   tomatoes, peeled, seeded
   and sliced
$\frac{1}{4}$ cup chopped parsley
salt and pepper
2 tablespoons butter
$\frac{1}{2}$ cup grated Parmesan cheese

Method
Brown the onion lightly in the oil, add the garlic, tomatoes and parsley and season well. Simmer gently for 15–20 minutes or until the mixture is soft and pulpy, stirring occasionally.

Cook the fettucine in plenty of boiling salted water for 6–8 minutes or until it is tender but still firm ('al dente'). Stir occasionally to prevent it from sticking. Drain it, rinse with hot water and return to the pan with the butter. Toss over heat until very hot.

Pile fettucine in a serving dish, spoon the tomato mixture on top, sprinkle with cheese and serve at once.

Parmesan cheese for pasta should be freshly grated so the flavor is at its best. Parmesan cheese in the piece is available in most supermarkets and specialty stores; Italian groceries often carry freshly grated Parmesan.

Lasagne or Canneloni Dough

$2\frac{1}{2}$ cups flour
$\frac{1}{2}$ teaspoon salt
$1\frac{1}{2}$ tablespoons olive oil
2 eggs, beaten to mix
3–4 tablespoons milk or water

Makes 20 canneloni (4 inch squares).

Method
Sift the flour with the salt onto a board or marble slab.

Make a well in the center and add the oil, eggs and milk or water. Start to draw the flour into the center, working the mixture together with the fingers of one hand. If necessary, add a little more milk or water, or more flour, to make a smooth dough that is soft but not sticky.

Knead the dough thoroughly for 5 minutes until it is very smooth and elastic. Cover and let stand 1 hour to lose some of its elasticity.

Roll out the dough as thinly as possible.

For lasagne, cut it into strips $1\frac{1}{2}$–2 inches wide and about 6 inches long.

For canneloni, cut it into 4–$4\frac{1}{2}$ inch squares.

Spread the dough on wax paper or paper towels and let stand at least 3 hours to dry.

For **green lasagne** (lasagne verde) or **green canneloni**: add 3 tablespoons spinach purée, cooked over low heat until very dry, to the eggs when mixing the dough and add only 2 tablespoons milk or water.

The **canneloni** and **lasagne** recipes in this feature serve 6 people as an entrée and 8 as an appetizer.

Lasagne Bolognese

$2\frac{1}{2}$ cup quantity of fresh
   lasagne dough
white sauce, made with $\frac{1}{4}$ cup
   butter, $\frac{1}{4}$ cup flour, $2\frac{1}{2}$ cups
   milk
$\frac{1}{2}$ cup grated Parmesan cheese

For bolognese sauce
3 tablespoons oil
1 medium onion, chopped
1 lb ground beef
4 tablespoons tomato purée
1 clove of garlic, crushed
$\frac{1}{2}$ cup stock
$\frac{1}{2}$ cup red wine
pinch of nutmeg
salt and pepper
1 cup ($\frac{1}{4}$ lb) chopped
   mushrooms

Large shallow baking dish

This dish can be made with plain or spinach-flavored lasagne.

Method
To make the bolognese sauce: in a saucepan heat the oil and fry the onion until soft. Stir in the beef and cook, stirring, until brown. Add the tomato purée, garlic, stock, wine, nutmeg and salt and pepper to taste and simmer the sauce over very low heat, uncovered, for 20 minutes or until thick, stirring occasionally. Add the mushrooms and cook 10 minutes longer.

Put the lasagne in a large pan of boiling salted water and simmer 8–10 minutes or until tender but still firm ('al dente'). Stir it occasionally to prevent it from sticking. Drain lasagne, rinse with hot water and spread on a damp cloth.

Make the white sauce and season well.

Butter the dish, spoon in a layer of bolognese sauce and cover with alternate layers of strips of lasagne and white sauce until all ingredients are used, ending with white sauce.

Sprinkle the top thickly with grated Parmesan cheese and bake in a moderately hot oven (375°F) for 15–20 minutes or until the lasagne is bubbling and brown.

Lasagne bolognese — the pasta is layered with meat sauce and white sauce

Lasagne Rustica

2½ cup quantity of fresh
   lasagne dough
3 cups tomato sauce
½ cup grated Parmesan cheese

For meat sauce
¼ lb salt pork, diced, blanched
   and drained
¾ lb lean ground pork
2 tablespoons butter
1 medium onion, chopped
1 carrot, chopped
1 stalk of celery, chopped
salt
black pepper, freshly ground
½ cup white wine
½ cup stock
bouquet garni

Large shallow baking dish

Method
To make the meat sauce: in a saucepan heat the butter, add the onion, carrot and celery and cook gently until the vegetables are soft. Add the salt pork and fry until browned. Stir in the ground pork, season and cook, stirring until the ground pork is browned. Add the wine, stock and bouquet garni and simmer, uncovered, for 15 minutes or until the sauce is well reduced and thick; stir occasionally. Remove bouquet garni.

Put the lasagne in a large pan of boiling salted water and simmer 8–10 minutes or until tender but still firm ('al dente'). Stir occasionally to prevent it from sticking. Drain the lasagne, rinse it with hot water and spread out on a damp cloth. Butter the dish.

Spoon a layer of meat sauce into the dish and cover with a layer of lasagne. Coat with tomato sauce, add more lasa-

gne and continue in this way until all ingredients are used, ending with a layer of tomato sauce.

Sprinkle the top thickly with grated Parmesan cheese and bake in a moderately hot oven (375°F) for 15–20 minutes or until bubbling and brown.

Tomato Sauce for Pasta

1 can (2 lb) Italian-type plum
   tomatoes
1 tablespoon tomato paste
2 tablespoons butter
2 tablespoons flour
2 cups stock
salt and pepper
1 bay leaf
1 clove of garlic, crushed

This recipe was first given in Volume 5. Makes about 5 cups.

Method
Melt the butter in a saucepan, stir in the flour and cook until straw-colored. Blend in the tomato paste and stock and stir until the mixture boils.

Add the tomatoes, crushing well with the back of a wooden spoon. Stir in the salt, pepper, bay leaf and garlic.

Cover pan and simmer 20–30 minutes or until the sauce is fairly thick. Work the mixture through a strainer into a bowl, taste for seasoning, then use as required.

Chicken Canneloni

2½ cup quantity of fresh
   canneloni dough
3 lb roasting chicken
1 onion, quartered
2–3 stalks of celery
1 carrot, quartered
bouquet garni
6 peppercorns
salt and pepper
mornay sauce, made with ¼
   cup butter, ¼ cup flour,
   2 cups milk, 1 teaspoon
   Dijon-style mustard, ½ cup
   grated Parmesan cheese
2 egg yolks
¾ cup light cream
¼ cup grated Parmesan cheese
¼ cup browned breadcrumbs

Large shallow baking dish

Method
Put the chicken in a kettle with the onion, celery, carrot, bouquet garni, peppercorns, 1 teaspoon salt and water to cover, add the lid and simmer 1 hour or until chicken is very tender. Cool it in the liquid until lukewarm, then drain and remove the meat from the bones, discarding the skin. Cut the meat into strips.

Cook the canneloni in a large pan of boiling salted water, adding only 8–10 squares at a time so they do not stick together, for 8–10 minutes or until the squares are tender but still firm ('al dente'). Stir them occasionally to prevent them from sticking. Drain the squares, rinse with hot water and spread them on a damp cloth.

Make the mornay sauce and season well, add half to the chicken strips with egg yolks and taste for seasoning.

Put about 2 tablespoons of chicken mixture on each square of pasta, roll loosely and arrange in buttered dish.

Add the cream to the remaining mornay sauce and reheat gently without boiling. Spoon the sauce over canneloni to coat and sprinkle with Parmesan cheese and breadcrumbs, mixed together. Bake canneloni in a moderately hot oven (375°F) 15–20 minutes or until bubbling and brown.

Semolina flour, made from hard durum wheat, is particularly good for making pasta as it has a high gluten content that makes the dough easy to work, and a high proportion of protein that prevents the starch from breaking down during cooking. This gives a firm, resilient pasta.

Semolina flour is available at Italian grocery stores. Substitute it directly for regular flour in these pasta recipes but allow 1–1½ tablespoons less liquid for every 2 cups semolina flour used.

In this lesson, terms like '3 cup quantity' refer to the amount of dough obtained by using 3 cups flour, not 3 cups prepared dough.

Stuffed canneloni verde is served with a spinach-flavored sauce

Canneloni Verde

1½ cup quantity of fresh canneloni dough (see page 118)
½ cup grated Parmesan cheese (for sprinkling)

For filling
1½ lb raw veal, ground
1½ cups béchamel sauce, made with 3 tablespoons flour, 3 tablespoons butter, 1½ cups milk (infused with slice of onion, 6 pepper-corns, 1 bay leaf and a blade of mace)
2 egg yolks
pinch of ground nutmeg
salt and pepper

For green sauce
1 cup cooked spinach purée
¼ cup butter
¼ cup flour
1½ cups milk
1 cup heavy cream

Large shallow baking dish

Method
To make the filling: make the béchamel sauce and cool. Stir in the veal, egg yolks, nutmeg and seasoning.

Cook the canneloni dough in a large pan of boiling salted water, adding only 8–10 squares at a time, so they do not stick together, for 8–10 minutes or until the squares are tender but still firm ('al dente'). Stir them occasionally to prevent them from sticking. Drain the squares, rinse them with hot water and spread on a damp cloth.

Put about 2 tablespoons filling on each square of pasta, roll up and arrange them in a large shallow buttered baking dish.

To make the green sauce: melt the butter, stir in the flour and when foaming, pour in the milk. Bring to a boil, stirring, and simmer 2 minutes. Add the heavy cream, nutmeg, seasoning and spinach purée, and bring just back to a boil. Taste for seasoning and spoon over the canneloni to coat.

Cover the dish and bake the canneloni in a moderate oven (350°F) for 45–50 minutes. Ten minutes before the end of cooking, remove the cover, sprinkle the canneloni with grated Parmesan cheese and continue cooking until the top is browned.

GNOCCHI

Gnocchi – a type of dumpling – are not really pasta but are included in this feature. There are three types – romana, made with cornmeal, parisienne, made with regular flour, and potato gnocchi, made with mashed potatoes. Any gnocchi can be served as the accompaniment to an entrée and gnocchi romana and parisienne are substantial enough to serve as an appetizer or as a light entrée for lunch or supper.

To shape gnocchi, dip the spoons in the water for poaching until hot; fill one spoon well with dough and smooth the top with the other spoon

Gnocchi Parisienne

1 cup flour
6 tablespoons butter
¾ cup milk
3 eggs
½ cup grated Parmesan cheese
pinch of dry mustard
salt and pepper
mornay sauce, made with 3 tablespoons butter, 3 tablespoons flour, 2 cups milk, 1 teaspoon Dijon-style or prepared mustard, ¾ cup grated Parmesan cheese
¼ cup grated Parmesan cheese (for sprinkling)

These gnocchi are made like choux pastry, and poached in water before being coated with mornay sauce. Then the dish is baked in the oven so the gnocchi puff up in the same way as choux pastry. Serves 6–8 people as an appetizer or 4 as an entrée.

Method
Sift the flour onto a sheet of wax paper.

Melt the butter in the milk, bring the mixture just to a boil, take from heat and add all the flour at once. Beat until the mixture is smooth and pulls away from the sides of the pan. Cool slightly, then beat in the eggs, one at a time, by hand or with an electric mixer. If the eggs are large, all of the last egg may not be needed, so beat it to mix and add it a little at a time to the dough.

When the right amount of egg has been added, the dough is glossy and falls easily from the spoon without being liquid. Stir in the cheese and add the mustard and seasoning to taste.
Note: at this stage the dough can be left, covered, for several hours or overnight. Once poached and coated with sauce it can also be left in the dish for several hours before it is baked.

To poach: heat a large pan of salted water. When just simmering, dip two soup spoons in the water until hot, then fill one spoon well with dough and smooth the top with the other spoon to form an oval. To make sure there are no cracks, dig down well into the dough to get a really heaping spoonful.

When shaped hold the spoon containing the mixture in just trembling water and tap the tip of the spoon gently on the bottom of the pan 2–3 times; the gnocchi will float off the spoon. The water must only tremble, not even simmer, or the gnocchi will break up. Continue until all the dough is used or until the pan is fairly full.

The gnocchi do not swell at this stage but they need room to be turned or to turn by themselves. Poach gnocchi 12 minutes after the last one was added. Shake the pan gently from time to time.

When the gnocchi are firm to the touch (they will look slightly spongy), lift them out with a slotted spoon and drain on paper towels. If any mixture remains, continue cooking until it is all used.

To bake gnocchi: arrange them in a large buttered shallow baking dish and set oven at hot (400°F). Make the mornay sauce, season well and coat gnocchi. Sprinkle with grated Parmesan cheese. Bake in heated oven for 30–40 minutes or until the gnocchi are well puffed and brown. Let stand in a warm place 5 minutes before serving; the gnocchi will subside slightly and have a better texture.

Gnocchi parisienne, coated with mornay sauce and grated cheese, are baked until they are well puffed and brown

Small Gnocchi

$\frac{3}{4}$ cup flour
$\frac{1}{4}$ cup butter
$\frac{1}{2}$ cup milk
2 eggs
6 tablespoons grated
    Parmesan cheese
pinch of dry mustard
salt and pepper
mornay sauce, made with
    2 tablespoons butter,
    2 tablespoons flour, 1$\frac{1}{2}$ cups
    milk, $\frac{1}{2}$ teaspoon Dijon-style
    or prepared mustard,
    6 tablespoons grated
    Parmesan cheese
$\frac{1}{2}$ cup cooked ham, cut in
    julienne strips, or 1 cup
    ($\frac{1}{4}$ lb) sliced mushrooms,
    cooked in 1 tablespoon
    butter (optional)

*Pastry bag and $\frac{1}{2}$ inch plain
tube (optional); 4 individual
gratin or baking dishes*

Method

Make the dough with the flour, butter, milk, eggs, cheese; mustard and seasoning as for gnocchi parisienne (see page 121).

To poach: heat a large pan of salted water. If using a pastry bag, put the dough into the bag, fitted with the $\frac{1}{2}$ inch tube. When the water is just trembling, rest the pastry bag on the edge of the pan. Dip a small knife into the water, then squeeze the pastry bag; as the dough comes out, cut it with the knife into $\frac{1}{2}$ inch lengths. Do this as quickly as possible so all the dough is added at the same time. If you have no pastry bag, shape small balls of dough with 2 teaspoons dipped in hot water as for gnocchi parisienne.

Shake the pan gently to separate the gnocchi, then poach 6—7 minutes or until very firm to the touch. Lift gnocchi out with a slotted spoon and drain on paper towels.

Make the mornay sauce and season well; set oven at hot (400°F).

Thoroughly butter the dishes and put a little of the ham or mushrooms in each, if you like. Arrange gnocchi on top and coat with mornay sauce. Bake in heated oven for 15—20 minutes or until gnocchi are well puffed and the tops are browned. Serve at once.

Potato Gnocchi

3 medium potatoes
1 tablespoon butter
$\frac{1}{4}$ cup flour
salt and pepper
1 egg, beaten to mix
$\frac{1}{4}$ cup melted butter (for
    serving)

Method

Peel and cook the potatoes in boiling salted water for 15—20 minutes or until tender. Drain them thoroughly and work through a wire sieve or potato ricer or crush with a potato masher. Cool slightly, beat in the butter, flour and seasoning and gradually add enough egg to bind the mixture without letting it become sticky.

When well mixed and smooth, roll the mixture with your hands on a floured board to a cylinder about $\frac{3}{4}$ inch thick. Cut into 1 inch pieces and roll each with the flat part of a fork into a ball.

To poach: heat a pan of salted water until it just trembles, add the gnocchi and poach 10—12 minutes or until firm. Lift gnocchi out with a slotted spoon, drain on paper towels and arrange in a hot serving dish. Spoon over melted butter and serve.

Gnocchi Romana

1 cup cornmeal or coarse
    semolina
1 medium onion
1 bay leaf
2 cups milk
2 cups water
salt and pepper
1 teaspoon Dijon-style mustard
6 tablespoons butter
3 egg yolks
1 cup grated Parmesan or
    Romano cheese
mornay sauce, made with
    2 tablespoons butter,
    2 tablespoons flour, 2 cups
    milk, 2 egg yolks, $\frac{1}{4}$ cup
    grated Parmesan cheese

Method

Put the onion, bay leaf, milk and water in a large saucepan, cover, bring to a boil and infuse 10 minutes. Discard the onion and bay leaf.

Stir the cornmeal or semolina into the seasoned milk mixture, bring to a boil, stirring; season and simmer, stirring often, for 7—10 minutes. The mixture should drop fairly easily from the spoon and not be sticky. If too thick, add more liquid.

Watchpoint: the amount of milk and water needed varies with the type and coarseness of the grain used.

Take from heat, stir in the mustard, half the butter, egg yolks and three-quarters of grated cheese; adjust seasoning. Pour the mixture into a buttered tray or shallow baking sheet and spread out to $\frac{1}{2}$—$\frac{3}{4}$ inch thickness. Cover and let stand 2—3 hours in refrigerator or overnight until firm.

Warm the tray or baking sheet lightly to melt the butter, turn gnocchi onto a flat surface and cut into small squares, rounds or crescents. Arrange these in a large well-buttered ovenproof dish with the pieces overlapping, leaving a slight well in the center. Sprinkle gnocchi generously with the remaining butter, melted.

Make the mornay sauce and spoon it into the center of the dish; sprinkle with the remaining cheese. Bake in a hot oven (400°F) for 10—15 minutes or until brown.

All the **Gnocchi** recipes on this page serve 6—8 people as an appetizer or 4 as an entrée.

Choose pizza napolitana or with shrimps (front left and right),
al prosciutto (center) or alla vongole (at back) – recipes are on pages 127–128

GIVE A PIZZA PARTY

Try giving a pizza party as an easy and amusing way to entertain a crowd. You can prepare the dough several hours — or even 2—3 days — ahead of cooking time; let it rise, then knead it, cover and store in a plastic bag in the refrigerator. Make the toppings in advance as well and choose several different ones for an exciting and colorful party spread.

When ready to use, pat out the dough, cover with topping and bake the pizza — again ahead of the time for the party. To serve, simply put them in a moderate oven (350°F) for 5—10 minutes so that guests can enjoy their pizza piping hot. Add one or two salads and some peaches in chianti and your menu is made.

Completed unbaked pizzas also freeze well; thaw them completely and let them rise before baking.

Individual pizzas are easy to serve for a party; the ones shown here are a variation of pizza con olive, with sliced pimiento added to the topping

Basic Pizza Dough

8 cups flour
2 teaspoons salt
about 1½ cups milk
2 packages dry or 2 cakes
compressed yeast
7 eggs, beaten to mix
1 cup butter, softened

This quantity of basic dough makes 4 pizzas, each serving 4–6 people. The following recipes are enough for 1 pizza only, unless otherwise specified.

Method

Sift the flour and salt into a warm bowl and make a well in the center. Warm the milk, pour into the well and sprinkle or crumble over the yeast. Let stand 5 minutes or until the yeast is dissolved, add the eggs, gradually stir in the flour and knead the mixture for 5 minutes or until it is smooth and elastic.

Work in the softened butter, cover and let rise in a warm place for 40 minutes or until doubled in bulk. Knead it lightly to knock out the air, cover the bowl with a damp cloth or plastic wrap and refrigerate 2–3 hours if not needed at once.

To shape pizza: divide the dough into four, knead each piece lightly on a floured board until smooth, then pat out to a 13–14 inch round on a floured baking sheet with the palm of the hand.
Note: a 13–14 inch flan ring placed around the pizza will keep the dough in shape and makes it easy to cover the entire surface with topping without it running over the sides and sticking to the baking sheet. If you make pizza in the regular way without a flan ring, make the circle of dough 1–2 inches

larger to let the topping spread without spilling over the sides.

Set oven at hot (400°F).

Cover the rounds of dough with any of the suggested toppings and let rise in a warm place for 10–15 minutes or until doubled in bulk. Bake in heated oven for 30–35 minutes or until the bread is lightly browned. Lift off the flan rings, if used, and slide the pizza onto a wooden board to serve.

Pat out pizza dough to size of the flan ring if using one

Spoon the prepared topping onto pizza dough and let rise 10–15 minutes or until doubled in bulk before baking

Individual Pizzas

For a party, small individual pizza make a pleasant variation. Any of the recipes in this feature can be used except calzone and pizza rustica. The quantities will make 4 individual pizzas, 7–8 inches in diameter.

Pizza with shrimps

2 cup quantity of basic pizza dough

For topping
1½ lb peeled uncooked medium shrimps
2 cups (½ lb) chopped mushrooms
4 shallots, finely chopped
1 cup white wine
¼ cup butter
3 tablespoons flour
1½ cups chicken stock
2 cloves of garlic, crushed
2 teaspoons tomato paste
4 tomatoes, peeled, seeded and cut in strips
salt and pepper

Method

Simmer the shallots in the white wine until reduced by half. Add the shrimps and mushrooms, cook very slowly for 5 minutes and reserve.

Melt the butter, stir in the flour and cook until straw-colored. Add the stock, garlic and tomato paste and stir until boiling. Cook 3–4 minutes, add to the shrimp mixture with the tomatoes and season. Spread the mixture on the pizza dough and let rise. Bake as for basic dough.

Pizza al Melanzane
(Eggplant Pizza)

2 cup quantity of basic pizza dough

For topping
1 large eggplant, sliced
6 tablespoons olive oil
2 onions, chopped
2 cloves of garlic, crushed
3 tomatoes, peeled, seeded and chopped or 2 cups (1 lb) canned Italian-type plum tomatoes, drained and lightly crushed
2 teaspoons oregano
salt
black pepper, freshly ground
¼ lb sliced Mozzarella cheese

Method

Sprinkle the eggplant slices with salt and let stand 30 minutes to dégorger (draw out the bitter juices). Rinse and dry the slices on paper towels.

In a skillet heat half the oil and brown the eggplant slices on both sides. Remove them, add the remaining oil and onions and fry until they are soft. Add the garlic, tomatoes, oregano and seasoning and cook, stirring, occasionally, until thick.

Arrange the eggplant slices, overlapping, on the pizza dough. Cover them with the tomato mixture and top with sliced cheese. Let rise, then bake as for basic dough.

Pizza Napoletana

2 cup quantity of basic pizza
dough (see page 127)

For topping
8–12 anchovy fillets
2–3 tablespoons milk
¼ cup olive oil
1 onion, finely chopped
6 ripe tomatoes, peeled,
seeded and sliced, or 4 cups
(2 lb) canned Italian-type
plum tomatoes, drained and
lightly crushed
½ lb sliced Mozzarella or
Bel Paese cheese
2 cloves of garlic, crushed
1 tablespoon marjoram or
basil
salt and pepper

Method
Cut the anchovy fillets in half
lengthwise and soak them in
the milk for 15 minutes to
remove excess salt. Drain.

Heat the oil in a skillet, add
the onion and fry until soft.
Stir in the tomatoes, cook 10
seconds, take from heat and
add the garlic, marjoram or
basil. Season to taste.

Spread the pizza dough
with the tomato mixture.
Cover with sliced cheese and
arrange a lattice of anchovy
on top. Let rise, then bake as
for basic dough.

Pizza al Prosciutto (Ham Pizza)

2 cup quantity of basic pizza
dough (see page 127)

For topping
1½ cups (¾ lb) cooked ham, cut
in strips
½ cup (¼ lb) mortadella
sausage, cut in strips
½ cup butter
2 large mild or Bermuda
onions, finely sliced
6 tablespoons chutney
salt
black pepper, freshly ground

Here, prosciutto normally
refers to very thinly sliced
raw ham, although the Italian
word prosciutto means any
kind of ham, raw or cooked.

Method
Melt the butter, add the
onions and cook over very low
heat until golden brown.
Add the ham and mortadella,
stir in the chutney and season.

Spread the mixture on
the pizza dough. Let rise, then
bake as for basic dough.

The name **Pizza** origin-
ated in the area around
Naples, Italy, but it is not
certain whether the name
comes from the nearby
village of Pizza because
the best grain for pizza
flour is found (and ground)
there.

A pizza may have been
made originally to use up
leftover bread dough and
tomato sauce, plus what-
ever sausage, ham or
cheese happened to be
available.

Pizza alle Vongole (Clam Pizza)

2 cup quantity of basic pizza
dough (see page 127)

For topping
6 ripe tomatoes, peeled,
seeded and sliced, or 4 cups
(2 lb) canned Italian-type
plum tomatoes, drained and
lightly crushed
¼ cup olive oil
1 onion, finely chopped
2 cloves of garlic, crushed
1 tablespoon marjoram or basil
salt and pepper

For clam sauce
2 quarts clams
2 tablespoons butter
1½ tablespoons flour
½ cup heavy cream
2 tablespoons chopped
parsley

13–14 inch flan ring

Method
Heat the oil in a skillet, add
the onion and fry until soft.
Stir in the tomatoes, cook 10
seconds, take from heat, add
the garlic, marjoram or basil
and season to taste.

Spread the pizza dough
with the tomato topping and
let rise 10–15 minutes or
until doubled in bulk. Bake
pizza in moderately hot oven
(375°F) for 30–35 minutes or
until lightly browned.

Meanwhile clean the clams
and cook them, covered, in a
little water over high heat
until they open; stir them
once. Take them from their
shells, discarding any which
do not open, and strain the
cooking liquid.

In a pan melt the butter,
stir in the flour and pour on
the cooking liquid and cream.
Bring to a boil, stirring, and
simmer 2 minutes. Season and

add the clams and parsley.

Spoon the clam sauce over
the hot pizza and serve at
once.

Pizza con Olive

2 cup quantity of basic pizza
dough (see page 127)

For topping
8–12 anchovy fillets
2–3 tablespoons milk
2 tablespoons olive oil
2 tomatoes, peeled, seeded
and chopped
1 clove of garlic, crushed
salt
black pepper, freshly ground
½ lb sliced Mozzarella cheese
½ cup small Italian or Nicoise
ripe olives, halved and
pitted
½ cup small Italian or Nicoise
green olives, halved and
pitted

Method
Cut the anchovy fillets in half
lengthwise, soak them in the
milk for 15 minutes to remove
excess salt and drain.

In a skillet heat the oil
and add the tomatoes, garlic
and seasoning; cook 5 minutes
or until the tomatoes are soft.

Spread the pizza dough with
the cheese and spread over
the tomato mixture with the
halved olives. Arrange the
anchovy fillets in a lattice
pattern on top and sprinkle
with black pepper. Let rise,
then bake as for basic pizza
dough.

Pizza con olive, made without a flan ring, has a crisp edge. A lattice pattern of anchovies tops the olive mixture

Pizza alle Salsiccie
(Sausage Pizza)

2 cup quantity of basic pizza
    dough (see page 127)

For topping
¾ lb fresh Italian sausage,
    thinly sliced
1 tablespoon oil
6 ripe tomatoes, peeled,
    seeded and sliced, or 4 cups
    (2 lb) canned Italian-type
    plum tomatoes, drained and
    lightly crushed
1 teaspoon basil
½ cup grated Parmesan cheese
salt
black pepper, freshly ground
    (optional)

Method
In a skillet heat the oil and
brown the sausage on both
sides. Add the tomatoes,
basil and cheese and cook
until thick. Cool, spread the
mixture over the dough and, if
using mild sausage, season
lightly. If using hot sausage,
omit pepper. Let rise; then
bake as for basic dough.

Pizza al Funghi
(Mushroom Pizza)

2 cup quantity of basic pizza
    dough (see page 127)

For topping
4 cups (1 lb) sliced mushrooms
½ cup olive oil
1 large mild or Bermuda
    onion, sliced
3 cloves of garlic, crushed
salt
black pepper, freshly ground
3 tablespoons chopped
    parsley
2 teaspoons basil

Method
Heat half the oil in a skillet
and sauté the onion until soft.
Add the remaining oil with
the mushrooms, garlic and
salt and pepper and cook 3—4
minutes until the mushrooms
are tender. Take from heat
and stir in the herbs.
    Spread the mushroom
mixture on the pizza dough.
Let rise, then bake as for
basic dough.

Pizza Rustica
(Country Pizza)

2 cup quantity of basic pizza
    dough (see page 127)

For filling
1 lb ricotta cheese or creamed
    cottage cheese
¼ cup grated Parmesan cheese
¼ lb ham or salami diced
2 eggs, beaten to mix
salt and pepper

10 inch pie pan

Pizza can also mean pie; this
dish is simply a country cheese
pie made with pizza dough.

Method
Divide the dough in half and
roll out one piece to line the
pie pan.
    Beat the eggs into both
the cheeses, add the ham or
salami with salt and pepper
to taste and spread the filling
on the pie.
    Roll out the remaining
dough to cover the pie, seal
the edges and let rise 10—15
minutes. Bake in a moderately
hot oven (375°F) for 45
minutes or until the top is
golden brown.

Peaches in Chianti go
well after pizza. Allow 1½
fresh peaches per person;
scald, peel, halve, pit and
slice them into a bowl.
Sprinkle sugar between
the layers. (If using canned peach slices, drain
and layer with only a little
sugar.) Pour over red
chianti wine to cover the
fruit and chill.

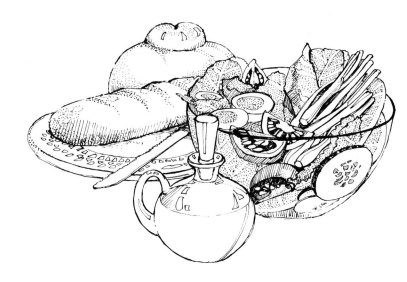

Pizza di Scammero
(Escarole Pizza)

2 cup quantity of basic pizza
dough (see page 127)

For topping
1 large head of escarole
8–12 anchovy fillets
2–3 tablespoons milk
2 tablespoons olive oil
1 clove of garlic, crushed
black pepper, freshly ground
salt
1 egg yolk
1 tablespoon capers
12–16 ripe Italian or Greek
olives, pitted and chopped
2 tablespoons golden raisins

Method
Cut the anchovy fillets in half
lengthwise and soak them in
the milk for 15 minutes to
remove excess salt. Drain
and chop.

Trim the base of the escarole, cut it in half and wash
thoroughly. Cook in boiling
salted water for 5–6 minutes,
drain, put escarole between 2
plates and squeeze out all the
water. Chop finely.

In a skillet heat the oil and
sauté the escarole with garlic,
pepper and a very little salt.
When tender, cool it and stir
in the egg yolk.

Divide the pizza dough in
half and pat one half out on a
baking sheet to a 10 inch
circle. Spread the escarole
mixture on top, leaving a ½
inch border, and spread the
anchovies, capers, olives and
raisins on top. Brush the
edge with water, pat out the
remaining dough to a 10 inch
round and place it on top,
sealing the edges firmly so the
filling cannot leak.

Let rise 10–15 minutes.
Bake in a hot oven (400°F)
40–45 minutes or until the
pizza bread is browned.

Calzone
(Cheese and Ham Turnovers)

2 cup quantity of basic pizza
dough (see page 127)

For filling
5–6 slices of Mozzarella or
Bel Paese cheese
5–6 slices of ham
olive oil (to sprinkle)
salt and pepper

*6 inch cookie cutter; fat
thermometer (optional)*

Makes 5–6 calzone.

Method
Roll out the dough very
thinly and cut into circles
with the cookie cutter. Cut
the ham and cheese into
smaller circles.

On each circle of dough,
lay a circle of cheese and a
circle of ham. Sprinkle over
a little olive oil and season to
taste. Brush the edges of the
dough with water and fold
up over the circles to form
turnover shapes. Press the
edges together to seal.

Let dough rise 10–15
minutes and bake the cal-
zone in a hot oven (400°F)
for 25–30 minutes or until
golden brown, or fry in deep
fat (350°F on a fat ther-
mometer). Drain calzone on
paper towels before serving.

MEASURING & MEASUREMENTS

The recipe quantities in the Course are measured in standard level teaspoons, tablespoons and cups and their equivalents are shown below. Any liquid pints and quarts also refer to U.S. standard measures.

When measuring dry ingredients, fill the cup or spoon to overflowing without packing down and level the top with a knife. All the dry ingredients, including flour, should be measured before sifting, although sifting may be called for later in the instructions.

Butter and margarine usually come in measured sticks (1 stick equals $\frac{1}{2}$ cup) and other bulk fats can be measured by displacement. For $\frac{1}{3}$ cup fat, fill the measuring cup $\frac{2}{3}$ full of water. Add fat until the water reaches the 1 cup mark. Drain the cup of water and the fat remaining equals $\frac{1}{3}$ cup.

For liquids, fill the measure to the brim, or to the calibration line.

Often quantities of seasonings cannot be stated exactly, for ingredients vary in the amount they require. The instructions 'add to taste' are literal, for it is impossible to achieve just the right balance of flavors in many dishes without tasting them.

Liquid measure	Volume equivalent
3 teaspoons	1 tablespoon
2 tablespoons	1 fluid oz
4 tablespoons	$\frac{1}{4}$ cup
16 tablespoons	1 cup or 8 fluid oz
2 cups	1 pint
2 pints	1 quart
4 quarts	1 gallon

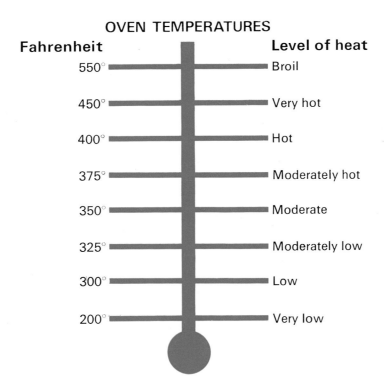

OVEN TEMPERATURES

Fahrenheit		Level of heat
550°		Broil
450°		Very hot
400°		Hot
375°		Moderately hot
350°		Moderate
325°		Moderately low
300°		Low
200°		Very low

OVEN TEMPERATURES AND SHELF POSITIONS

Throughout the Cooking Course, oven temperatures are stated in degrees Fahrenheit and in generally agreed levels of heat such as 'high' and 'moderate'. The equivalents are shown on the table above.

However, exact temperature varies in different parts of an oven and the thermostat reading refers to the heat in the middle. As the oven temperature at top and bottom can vary as much as 25°F from this setting, the positioning of shelves is very important. In general, heat rises, so the hottest part of the oven is at the top, but consult the manufacturer's handbook about your individual model.

Pans and dishes of food should be placed parallel with burners or elements to avoid scorched edges.

When baking cakes, there must be room for the heat to circulate in the oven around baking sheets and cake pans; otherwise the underside of the cakes will burn. If baking more than one cake in an oven that has back burners or elements, arrange the cakes side by side. If the oven has side burners, arrange cakes back and front.

Oven thermostats are often inaccurate and are unreliable at extremely high or low temperatures. If you do a great deal of baking or question the accuracy of your oven, use a separate oven thermometer as a check on the thermostat.

Cooking Curiosities

Stew pots can hold some pretty funny things. Think of any fish, animal or fowl, and it's likely that somewhere in the world someone is stewing it.

Some books carry recipes for stewing bear, squirrel, raccoon, muskrat, opossum and beaver, whose tail, it seems, should be kept for charcoal grilling. There is also a recipe, that was brought from China, for stewing Rocky Mountains' wildcat in whiskey; it is said to increase virility, but perhaps that depends on who gets more of the broth!

Chinese cuisine, thought by some to be unsurpassed in sophistication, has numerous recipes for snakemeat, including stews and soups. This last is said to be delicious as a consommé in which the snakes float or lie whole and skinned.

(Volume 8)

B

A

C

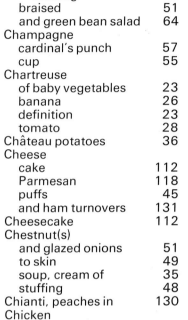

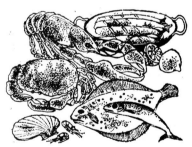

Acknowledgments
Photographs by Fred J.
Maroon on pages 11, 58, 66
and 98. Other photographs by
Michael Leale, Roger Phillips
and John Ledger. Photograph
on page 14 by Angel Studios;
on page 84 by Pictor.

NOTES

Notes

Notes